STEALTH EMAIL SECRETS

The Simplest System Ever Created For Writing High-Converting, Cash-Producing Emails On Command

By Conor Kelly

Table Of Stealthy Contents

Introduction – Why Email Marketing? ...Page 7

Chapter 1 – Of Sales Letters...Page 17

Chapter 2 – The Art Of The Lead Magnet...Page 39

Chapter 3 – The Customer Prototype...Page 44

Chapter 4 – Researching Your Market...Page 47

Chapter 5 – Writing Emails That Convert...Page 57

Chapter 6 – Biggest Email Myths & Mistakes...Page 94

Chapter 7 – Creating Offers That Compel Response...Page 105

Chapter 8 – Key Drivers Of Action...Page 116

Chapter 9 – Tips For Writing...Page 126

Chapter 10 – More Best Practices...Page 132

Bonus Chapter – How To Hire A Copywriter...Page 142

ABOUT YOUR MUSCULAR AUTHOR

Conor Kelly, a.k.a. The Muscle is a leading copywriter, email marketing specialist, and publisher of the "Small Business Marketing" Newsletter. A twelve-year direct-response marketing veteran, Conor has created email campaigns and sales letters that have translated to millions of dollars in sales for his clients. His methods have been proven in many different industries: health and fitness, chiropractic, wellness, personal development and success training, baseball coaching, Google ads for attorneys, computer services, and manufacturing.

Conor's emails are currently being read by people all over Canada, The U.S.A., Europe, and Africa. He specializes in helping small business owners, authors, speakers, and coaches sell more products and services, books, courses, and high-ticket coaching programs.

For more information, please visit www.ConorKelly.com where he publishes free daily marketing tips.

WHAT OTHER PEOPLE ARE SAYING ABOUT CONOR KELLY

"I've used copywriters in the past but was never happy with the results. It felt like I was overcharged for something that looked like a swipe job or a fill-in-the-blanks template. Also, it always took longer than I thought it should. With Conor, it's been the complete opposite. His fees are fair, the work is done quickly and it's very high-quality. Plus, he asks the right questions so I know he's doing his research! Highly recommend."

– **Matt Morse**, *Best-Selling Author & Business Coach*, www.Matt-Morse.com

"I am INCREDIBLY impressed with your content…it's in MY voice, and ACCURATE!!!"

— **Stephen Bach**, *The Digital Docs*, www.TheDigitalDocs.com

"I've been working with Conor on the sales page for my membership site and he's been outstanding. I've probably learned more from working with him on this project than in all the other marketing resources I've studied over the years. (Yeah, he's that good.) Which is why I recommend you to get on a call with him sooner rather than later!"

— **John "Coach Bru" Brubaker**, *Best-Selling Author & Keynote Speaker*, www.CoachBru.com

"I've worked with various copywriters over the course of 20 years of being in business. Some were expensive, some highly recommended, others had sterling reputations, yet at every turn I was disappointed.

Working with Conor has been a breath of fresh air. Not only has the entire process been professional from start to finish, but it quickly became obvious that he took the time to understand, I mean *really* understand our product, which caught me by surprise because I wasn't used to it!

For anyone who is thinking about working with Conor, I suggest you get on the phone with him. You'll have a different experience of a copywriter. I certainly did. And we'll continue our professional relationship into the foreseeable future."

— **Paul Reddick**, *Podcast Host & Leading Baseball Business Owner*, www.PaulReddickBaseball.com

"I gave Conor a tough assignment to help kickstart both my business and personal email campaigns. I was stuck and I needed professional help. He hit a home run with both assignments. He took the time and learned as much as he could about my businesses. His focused messaging with punchy copy was exactly what I needed to bring my engagement levels to record highs. I would strongly recommend Conor!"

— **Jon S. Rennie**, *Business Leader, Author, & Speaker*, www.JonSRennie.com

"I absolutely love reading your emails.......well written, creative, witty, informative, attention holding and overall a good read on this dreary Sunday afternoon."

–Debbie Augustt-Moffatt

"Conor hooked me on an opportunity to truly reach my existing patients and the rest of my decent sized list with more impactful, inspiring, and call-to-action language and content via e-mail. It's been almost 5 months, and the partnership is only growing. Conor is both responsive to our need for communication, eloquent with his language and leadership, and the impact it's had has only increased week by week. The value is great, as is the rapport. Thanks Conor!"

–Dr Josh Gelber, *Annex Family Chiropractic*

"With just a few short questions Conor was able to come up with a marketing plan that's perfectly customized to my goals and my strengths. He's very knowledgeable, and has great instincts!"

–**Amirali Rahnamoon**, *Osteopath at IN and OUT Fitness*

"I really enjoyed reading your book. It is very informative and has a good flow, which makes it easy to absorb all the valuable tips and tricks. It is also very relatable as the content can be applied to pretty much any type of business. You are a great writer and your sense of humour and clever wit kept me entertained and had my attention from start to finish. GREAT JOB!"

-- **Kathryn Evdokimova**, *Real Estate Salesperson*

"I liked Conor's writing a lot. It led to appointment bookings and sales of orthopaedic pillows fast! It contained relevant, accurate content that educated my patients and strengthened their relationship with the Clinic.

Conor is a knowledgeable and supportive professional. He quickly identified my needs and was responsive to them.

The bottom line: Conor's marketing services helped me to engage my current patients and resulted in more appointment bookings and health product sales. I would highly recommended him."

-- **Dr. Kevin Arnold**, BSc(Hon), EHC, DC, *Chiropractor to Elite Athletes*

Introduction

Why Email Marketing?

"Sometimes what we think we know blinds us to what we need to know."

-- Conor Kelly

I started marketing myself with email in 2007.

At the time, I was a personal trainer. I'd just started learning direct-response marketing. "The money's in the list," I heard. And I took it to heart. So I told all my clients I was starting a weekly email newsletter and asked them if they wanted to be on the list.

I got great feedback on my emails, but my list was very small.

Fast-forward to 2008.

I met a chiropractor who wanted a personal trainer at her clinic. We created a kind of joint venture relationship in which I would do the marketing and manage the personal training. The clinic had a subscriber list of about 10,000 because the business had been around for quite some time. So what I did was design a "no frills" basic offer page. It was a sort of low-tech, one-page site with an invite to her patients for a free consultation. And I crafted three emails to send to her email list. The clinic hadn't even been doing email particularly well. They'd sort of hit them once a month with one of these cheesy newsletters that nobody reads.

That first month, we notched up $14,000 in additional revenue for the clinic.

And that was it.

A light bulb went off in my head.

I went, *holy crap*. All you really need is a list on one end (ideally one that looks like Gary Halbert's "starving crowd") and a means to talk to them on the other. And that's really what email marketing is in a nutshell: your customers and prospects receiving your offers in a way that's intensely personal, a format they enjoy...and perhaps most importantly, have *chosen* to receive. The crazy thing is...

So Many Business Owners Are Sitting On A <u>Goldmine</u> And Don't Even Know It!

What is that gold mine?

Their customer list.

Even small "bricks and mortar" businesses like spas, training studios, hair salons, and yes, attorneys sometimes have lists of 5K-10K emails that they seldom or never communicate with. Take note...**everything's moving online.** Heck, people are even ordering groceries from Amazon now. And online...email is *king*. No other medium on the world wide web is putting more sales into spreadsheets than email. Any business owner that's not regularly in their customers' inbox is leaving a lot of money on the table.

Email's been my go-to since 2007.

(In fact, I have readers who have been with me since then, and still read my emails, which is pretty amazing to me.)

I see no reason why any local business with a list size like the above couldn't add at least 100K, probably more, to their bottom line this year, with email done right. That's pure profit. For an online-based business with a good product/service mix, or a speaker/author with back end coaching programs, a sound email marketing strategy can be worth MILLIONS over the course of a year.

I'm a 12-year direct-response marketing veteran and freelance copywriter specializing in email campaigns and sales letters.

Some of my recent successes include:

- ✓ Generating **10K in contracts** for a tech start up **from a single 10-word email** (I know that sounds crazy, but it's 100% true…and easy to do when you know what your market wants)
- ✓ **Doubling online conversions** of a women's fitness bootcamp
- ✓ **Adding 100K annual revenue** to a personal training studio without any additional advertising

More importantly for you:

The system I'm revealing for the first time here can drive…

A Massive Increase In Profits!

Almost immediately, in fact.

For any business with a reasonably sized list.

When email is done correctly…

It Connects You To You Customers.

It's more personal than social media.

I'll be honest, I'm of the mind that many small biz owners have been "conned" by social media companies promising the moon. For most, it's naught more than time and energy quicksand that sucks in the helpless and spits out their weary remains.

While Facebook claims 2 Billion accounts, a full 25% of those are fake. Email, on the other hand, boasts a hefty 6.32 Billion active accounts, making it ***5x bigger than Facebook***. I could also point out that many people go days without checking their social media, yet the average person checks their email multiple times per day. If I really wanted to make a statement I could add that 60% of business owners rate email as their most profitable marketing channel, more than all the various social media sites combined.

All that would be 100% true.

But the #1 reason to build a thriving email list?

You OWN your list.

It's yours.

You can download that sucker and re-upload it somewhere else. You can communicate with your list in the manner of your choosing. There's no one who can tell you otherwise. And there's no one who can take your list away from you. You don't own your social media followers. If that's all you've got – you're one policy update away from dead.

Case in point, five years ago I was getting most of the leads for my personal training biz from Google Adwords. One fine day, Google up and suspended my account. In order to reactivate it, I needed to add an asterisk with the words "results may vary" under each of the dozens of REAL before-and-after pics and testimonials displayed on my site.

Not only did this make my site look silly…

It sent my conversion rate spiraling down the drain.

And the leads all but dried up.

De-platforming is happening with frightening regularity. What's to stop Instagram from following Google's lead and saying e.g. "we don't like weight loss products…too scammy," then making the rules harder for an entire category of health-related marketers? An email list – especially a responsive one – is an asset. Arguably the best asset you can have.

But the best part, and this is what I really want to drive home to you, is that with email you are in their inbox because they've chosen for you to be there. They've subscribed. They're interested in what you have to offer. And so it's a totally different dynamic.

I was recently interviewed for a podcast and the host asked me to compare and contrast email marketing v. Facebook marketing. I said the key difference is your email subscribers have *agreed* to get promotional offers from you. In that sense, it's "consensual".

Both parties are in on the dance.

On any social media, you're *interrupting* whatever else it is they're there to do. Thus, folks are less likely to be open to it. We've all been the subject of unwelcome marketing advances, be they ads invading our social media feeds, spam, or telemarketing.

Being a welcome guest in your prospect's inbox is another animal altogether. It all but…

Eliminates Price Resistance!

That's what I find almost poetic about it.

That's because it helps your positioning with your customers. Allow me to explain. Your positioning or "selling posture", is the acid test that will propel to high profits in your business…**if** you get it right. I discovered the power of this in my personal training career when I started charging premium rates.

My goal was to focus on driving new business vs. training existing clients, which my team could do quite ably. But I did most of the sales consultations. Therefore, I'd almost always get requests from people who wanted me to train them. And for the most part, I didn't want to. After politely explaining I'm not really taking on new clients – at least not personally – I'd say, "but if you want, I can make an exception...it'll cost you $125 per session."

(An average rate for us at the time was $90 per session, already at the high end of our local market.)

Keep in mind I was trying to STEER THEM AWAY from training with me, and toward working with one of my staff. To my surprise, many folks still signed with me at the higher rate. I'd inadvertently created a dynamic of scarcity of, well, me. If you can convince a prospect that there's more demand for your service than you're able to fulfill, all the negotiating power shifts to you. You've established a 'seller's market' in which your lovely self can sit back and collect mucho dinero.

You see, we're *genetically wired* to assign a higher value to things we perceive as rare.

I can't tell you how many times telling someone I might NOT train them caused them to push back harder.

In email marketing, here's how this works:

The prospect has a problem. They search and find you. Or let's say one of your joint venture partners whose list they're already on emails them about joining your list. Either way, you've enticed them with "bait" to join your free email list. When they're ready, they call you...the expert. Now you're asking all the questions. You've made them the pursuer. Result? 1. New clients to you (the ones you *choose* to work with). 2. Me = happy.

See why I love this stuff?

But Isn't Email Dead?

Good question.

Recently I was at one of my favorite boutique coffee shops. I like the owners. I like the place. And I noticed they're not as busy as they could be. So I said to one of them, "Why don't you offer everyone who comes in 10% off their tab in exchange for their email address, which you'll use to send them exclusive discounts. Then, let me help you bring them in more often." His first question back to me was, "email, huh…but what do you think is coming next? What's the next big 'marketing thing'?"

Like what? You have some examples? Video conferencing, video chat, text chat, chat bots, live chat, text messaging, social media, Facebook messenger, What's App…all those things are already here. And email is still going strong. Email is pervasive, global, and foundational to the way we communicate as culture. And it will be for the foreseeable future.

Besides, this question misses the point.

I'm showing you how to bring in more business RIGHT NOW. What does it matter what might be around the corner at some hypothetical future date? Your customers are on email TODAY. And it costs you nothing to promote to them that way. The only legit excuse for not using email is you don't like making money.

More:

I find many business owners have this blind spot when it comes to their marketing. Another example…the first thing I ask new clients to do when they sign up is make a list of warm contacts with similar but non-competitive businesses we can co-promote with. For a chiropractor, it might be the personal training studio located nearby. Often they're surprised when they realize all the contacts they have but aren't leveraging.

Call it shiny object syndrome…

I call it *marketing myopia.*

It's that shortsightedness that afflicts all of us every now and again when we're busy doing what we do. What opportunities might you be missing? I hope this book will throw the shades open a lay them bare in the brightest afternoon sun. And I hereby challenge you to keep an open mind until I'm finished.

Mirror Selfies And The End Of Civilization

Meet Lazar Angelov.

He's Facebook's premier Bulgarian fitness model/personal trainer. I've never met him, but coincidentally he trains at the same gym I sometimes frequent when I'm in Sofia.

In "Fakebook" terms, his following is HUGE. His marketing basically consists of posting wax 'n tan shirtless pics of himself in various locales. This daily ab-check garners hundreds of thousands of likes, and thousands of comments.

(Isn't that one of the signs of the apocalypse?)

Besides foreshadowing our impending doom as a species, it's a pretty good racket. He's got a great physique and a photogenic look which seems to be enough for him to build a fan base he can besiege with his online personal training programs. Not hashing Lazar's gig. It works for him. And the audience he appeals to would rather watch his body talk than read his emails – which I can vouch for having read his emails.

Here's the point:

Prize poodle though he be on social media's hierarchy of "hotness", he still needs to pull people off Facebook (and get their email addy) to sell to them. And he does. His posts often include a link to his free report with a call to action. Unless I miss my guess, based on the size of his following he's doing a pretty penny selling e-books with badly written emails. Now if he had *good* copy...

Here's point #2:

If you've got any kind of consistent traffic, whether it's a social media following or a physical location that gets foot traffic, it's quick and easy to build an email list you can nurture to create more loyal customers and a near instant surge in cash flow. A list that can't be de-platformed, de-ranked, banished or otherwise taken away from you.

Last but not least, email marketing...

Attracts <u>other</u> marketing opportunities!

I often talk about its other less obvious benefits.

For one client (a software solution that lets health providers do home visits and manage scheduling, billing, and charting through the app) I sent out an email a while back that got a very interesting response. It turned out the head of alumni relations with the Canadian Chiropractic College was on the list, and he wanted to talk about offering the client's service to thousands of chiropractors across the country. We've since inked a partnership...one that will likely be worth tens of thousands over the next few years.

You never know who's listening.

When you're consistently "putting yourself out there" and demonstrating your leadership each day or each week in your emails, it makes you magnetic to opportunity. Over the years I've gotten referrals, requests for speaking engagements, overtures for lucrative joint ventures…all because someone forwarded one of my emails, or someone "unexpected" was already on my list.

It doesn't happen every day.

But it *does* happen.

The key is you can't be boring. Your emails must offer interest, humor, valuable content, inspiration or all of the above. In short, they must be *forwardable*. This book will show you – in the simplest of terms – how to do exactly that.

Your Customers Are In Search Of <u>Leadership</u>

What is your mission?

How much do you care about your customers?

It's my contention that if you want the best for them, you need to be in their inbox regularly (if not frequently) with great content that adds value while teasing your solutions, and demonstrates not only your expertise, but your leadership. It will do you well to note: people listen to experts, but they follow leaders. If you can help, it is your <u>duty</u> to do so.

This book will present what, in my clearly biased opinion, is probably the #1 way to set yourself apart and establish yourself as the go-to person in your niche or industry.

Don't get into email thinking about what you can get. If you really want to do email marketing well you **lead with a <u>giving</u> hand**. And so I think the basis of all good email marketing is really caring about your subscriber list, understanding their problems and wanting what's best for them.

I really couldn't make it any simpler.

Chapter 1

Of Sales Letters

"So the sales letter-writer, particularly when doing long-form copy, is in a battle for survival…and that battle is literally sentence by sentence, paragraph by paragraph." – Dan Kennedy

I know what you're thinking.

Isn't this a book about email marketing? Why in God's name would you lead with a chapter about sales letters?

Here's why:

When I first hung up my shingle as a copywriter I wanted to be an email specialist. I've been doing email marketing consistently since 2007. It's been my bread and butter. So it seemed like a natural fit. What I quickly realized, is that if I don't have a high-quality sales page, offer page, or sales letter to link to, I'm not going to be able to convert many sales.

And that's the point.

You can have the cleverest (even brilliant) high-converting emails, but…

The Sales Letter Is Where The Rubber Meets The Road!

That is, when it comes to converting traffic to customers.

If you ain't a got a good one, those hot little emails can still fall flat in the sales department.

Now, many local businesses or service businesses have a different type of offer. The typical chiropractic office (and I work with several) for example, can do well with a call to action as simple as "reply to this email" or "call the office" to book. When I work with authors, speakers, or coaches on the other hand, they're typically looking to "move" products, memberships, courses, or events.

For products and courses, you ideally want a sales letter that captures your prospect's attention, reels 'em in, and sells them on why they should take action **today**. This can take many forms; a sales letter, video sales letter, webinar, etc. I quickly figured out that if I wanted to help my email clients get results, I had to also write their sales letters. So I do.

Note:

Email done well can cover a lot of the heavy lifting when it comes to selling your products and courses. That's because you're consistently in front of your subscribers, demonstrating your value, showing yourself to be a thought leader in your niche, and delivering them content they love. Make a solid offer to a highly-qualified list that already knows, likes and trusts you…and you can often get away with bouncing them directly to a shopping cart. I've done it. I know plenty of marketers who have done it. But that's lazy. I still think you want a sales page.

Why not go for "optimal" vs. just taking what you can easily get?

The above is why this chapter is designed to give you some best practices and a few elements you might want to include for creating a sales letter.

Caveat:

This is a brief overview of an exhaustive topic. Whole books and courses could be written and indeed have been written about it. It's a subject I continue to study daily. To any copywriter that is serious about the profession, it's like flossing. So take these tips for what they are. If nothing else, they'll give you a starting point and help you avoid the mistakes many people make.

We begin with writing…

Headlines That *Demand* Your Prospect Drop Everything They're Doing And Give Your Message Their Undivided Attention!

The headline is one of the key elements of any sales letter (or any page, really).

Its job is to capture the reader's interest and make them want to read the first paragraph. Nothing else. You're not trying to sell at this point. You just want your prospect to read on. There's an art and a science to writing headlines. The best copywriters spend years honing this one skill. At its simplest level a headline speaks to the self-interest and curiosity of your potential buyer.

And what are people interested in?

Things they care about.

This comes back to doing your research and knowing your market (something we cover a bit more in chapter 4). Once armed with this hard won intel, here's a simple formula to follow for creating a headline that's pretty reliable:

[Your Main Credential Here] Reveals How To [Thing They Want #1], [Thing They Want #2], [Thing They Want #3], Without [Thing They Don't Want]!

Simple.

Here's an example of this puppy in action:

Chiropractor to Olympians & Pro Athletes Reveals How to Diagnose & Fix <u>Any</u> Health Issue or Injury, Without Uncomfortable Tests, Medications, Or Surgeries!

As you can see, it's not always exactly three benefits vs. one thing your market hates.

It can be one BIG benefit minus three things they hate. The ratio is always different. What's important here is the concept of speaking to their self-interest more than merely following a rote formula. The credential is what we call "proof". This is important because it lays the groundwork for the reader to accept your claims. In the example above, he's not just any old chiropractor, he works with *Olympians and Pro Athletes*. These are clients with high expectations who only work with the best. You don't get "the call" unless you're good or proven in some way.

There are obviously many more ways of doing this. Indeed, I could write an entire book just on headlines (maybe I will). But this formula is one of my go-to's. Use it (and it's not hard), and you'll do just fine.

Now, once you've got their attention, you're going to need to keep it with…

A Pulse-Pounding "Lead" That Crawls Inside The Reader's Brain, And Won't Let Them Turn Away!

I'm going to sound like a bit of a broken record here…

But entire books have been written on writing effective leads.

For our purposes, this does not need to be complicated. The lead builds on the momentum you created with that attention-grabbing headline. In a nutshell, the lead can be a short paragraph or two, rife with the prospect's self-interest, that tells them why they should read the rest of your lovely sales page. Your headline got them to read your first paragraph. Now your first paragraph should get them locked in to wanting to read your letter.

That's the game, by the way:

Get interest.

Keep it.

Line by line.

The quote that opened this chapter was from marketing legend and one of the world's highest paid copywriters, Dan Kennedy. It bears repeating. Here it is again:

> *"So the sales letter-writer, particularly when doing long-form copy, is in a battle for survival...and that battle is literally sentence by sentence, paragraph by paragraph."*

Your first few words better earn their place!

Here's the **simplest formula I know** for writing a kickass opening paragraph:

> If you would like to [main benefit of your product or service you know your prospect wants]...without [main thing your prospect hates]...then this brief letter/guide/report will show you how.

Going back to my chiropractor client, you can see how I've done this:

If you'd like a simple process for **healing faster, getting out of pain**, and **fixing any nagging health issues...**_without_ resorting to surgeries or medication, then this special report will show you how 12,785 of my patients have done it.

And how you can do it too, using the information in this report.

Now in this version I've added an ingredient which is particularly intoxicating to most prospects, which is even more proof. You see, not only will this letter show you how to do it...it will show you how *12,785 of my patients have done it.* It's not just a simple process. By implication, it's proven. This is a powerful way of weaving proof into your claims you'll do well to master.

As you can see, there's not much room for embellishment here. Less is more. The key is to use the right words to hook in your reader, and get them eager to read on.

Next up:

How you can...

Create A *Raging* Desire For Your Product Or Service With Stories, Credibility And/Or Interesting Mechanisms!

There are a number of ways we can go about this.

It really all comes back to your offer, market and overall game plan of what you're trying to achieve with this particular page. The idea is, we're about to drop some "hella cool" bullets and benefits on them, but before we do, we MUST set the stage. This could be its own book.

(Hmm, where have I heard that before?)

But to give you the leg up on the simplest way to do this…per my promise at the outset…there are only **three** you should care about.

Here we go:

1. The Magic Of Getting *Them* To Believe

A while back I had a consultation.

During the call it came out that one of the owners of the business had some pretty unique experience related to the product they were selling. In fact, I'd go as far as to say he's so uniquely qualified to do this sort of thing, that if you were in their market and you knew about him, you'd never consider going anywhere else.

Yet, these credentials were buried at the bottom of the page.

I didn't even see them at first.

This comes back to what marketing genius and all-time copywriting great Gary Halbert taught about why you must "prepare people to believe". You see, we learn that selling is about benefits. People buy the hole, not the drill – and all that jazz. So that's what many business owners do…throw a bunch of benefits on the page with an order button.

And that can work to some extent.

But without context…your benefits won't have anywhere near the same ability to tug at your prospect's wallet. Per Gary The Great…you've got to prepare people to believe your claims. And until you have their *belief*, you won't command their attention. Your prospect could feel pretty "meh" regarding your offers at that point…a dire situation for any salesperson.

Remember:

Belief is like *oxygen* to your copy.

Start with why they should believe you…

And never leave a benefit stranded.

One thing:

Overdo credibility and it can *cost* you sales. There's a delicate balance to be observed here that the best copywriters know how to push and pull on like a seductive dance. If all you do is flex your credentials, you can lose connection with your audience, which is also important. Don't build your podium so high that you're out of reach.

In general, I like to do some kind of "proof paragraph" between my opener and whatever I'm getting into whether it's a story or the offer or a unique mechanism of some kind. Then more proof after. Like a proof sandwich. Delicious.

2. Your "How".

The "mechanism" is how you deliver the results you deliver.

Especially if there's something unique or interesting about it, it pays to plug it into your sales copy – literally. One example off the top of my head is a success trainer I worked with who claimed to be able to rapidly "program" confidence into you.

There are a lot of personal development courses that promise to change your life overnight. It would be easy for a person's inner-skeptic to discount that particular claim. In this case, the client was a trained hypnotist. As such, he could put you into a trance and "suggest" to your subconscious that you ARE confident in the same way he could suggest someone was a chicken and they'd cluck like a chicken (a demonstration he ably used during his sales presentations to ramp up credibility even more).

It's not a unique promise.

But it's definitely a unique mechanism.

Going back to the chiropractor I referenced in the previous chapter, it was a diagnostic test he'd invented that allowed him to make the rather "out there" claim of being able to identify and fix *any* health issue. The test itself was a muscle test that could be performed on any pair of muscles, making it simple and repeatable, and therefore easy to confirm the test's results. This allowed him to plug in and "talk" to your nervous system, like a mechanic plugs into your car's onboard computer.

Sure enough, I routinely watched him produce INSTANT and DRAMATIC results. He even knew things you didn't think a chiropractor should be able to diagnose, such as when the patient had a viral infection. It got him the call to be the official chiropractor for athletes trying out for *The Canadian Olympic Track & Field Team.*

To my knowledge no other chiropractor has a method that's anything like this.

Talking about your method is a juicy way to stir up curiosity and interest for what you have to offer. Folks will be more open to your claims if it's some new mechanism THAT CAN BE MADE TO MAKE SENSE…sound enticing…and perhaps more importantly, make your claims seem more plausible and believable.

Speaking of which, another way to infuse your copy with belief and almost instantly elicit enormous desire for your product out of thin air is by using the power of…

3. An Imagination-Capturing Story!

Once upon a time…

I was tasked to write a JV email for a client.

(This is a cross-promotional email in which the client would promote a friendly, non-competitive business to his subscriber list in exchange for the same courtesy in return. It's basically a "I scratch your back, you scratch mine" scenario in which the client and the referral partner each sends an email promoting the other to their respective list.)

The JV partner was a women's fitness expert. As I looked at the promo page, I discovered something very interesting. She was a former fitness competitor who suffered a stroke while still in her thirties. This made her realize how the years of extreme diets and hard core workouts had been negatively impacting her health.

So she went back to school to become a holistic nutritionist.

Now, she uses this knowledge (and her own experience) to help women regain control of their bodies and their health…showing them a balanced, fun, and wellbeing-enhancing way to lose weight while leaving behind the crash diets and other foolishness.

That's a heck of a story.

Yet I had to scroll down to the bottom of the page to find it.

You see…

Stories Increase Desire For Your Product.

That's because they provide both *vision* and *context*.

Throughout the 8 years or so that I marketed my personal training business, my own story of transformation (and having been fat before) was at the forefront of everything I did. It was front and center on my website. I'd lead with it in all my public speeches. I'd meet people ten years later who'd tell me, "I never forgot your story." That's why, especially if you have a good one (or even a plain one you can "soup up") you'd have to be either a fool or mad as a bag of ferrets not to use it at every opportunity.

Our brains are hardwired to be persuaded by stories.

(Did you notice how I began a section on stories by telling a story?)

Stories have been the basis for communication on our culture going back thousands of years. Memory courses teach you if you want to remember something, put it in story form. From what I understand from reading and talking to neuroscientists, the ideal brain state for both retention of information and motivated action is one of *integration.*

Integration is when both the right and left sides of the brain are engaged. Stories are ideal for this because they're catnip to the creative, visual, and emotional right brain, and offer up a logical sequence of events to follow for the left brain. It probably hasn't occurred to you that helping your client 'integrate' both sides of his/her brain is how you make sales.

But this game-changing stealth tactic is so ninja, ninjas can't even wrap their kimonos around it.

It begins with understanding an ancient truth…

People buy based on EMOTION, and justify their decision with LOGIC.

Good one to remember.

Awareness of the body, emotion, and autobiographical memory are the domain of the right hemisphere of the brain. Logic, words, list and sequences, on the other hand, pertain more to the workings of the left brain. The principle of integration allows each side of the brain to function as they were intended to, while working in harmony to provide balance between the various aspects of our character. A person in the midst of an emotional breakdown has been hijacked by their right brain. A person operating mostly from the left lacks the larger emotional and physical context needed to fully appreciate the nuances of his/her current situation.

Your goal in telling a story is to bridge the gap.

In so doing, you elicit from the right brain the raw emotion, while the left provides a logical order to things. And you help them make sense of what they're feeling. Only then is the brain fully integrated. That's when all the ingredients needed for a successful completion to the sale are present. They'll intuitively understand the context in which your offering is useful to their lives. And they can "see themselves" in the frame of the picture you are creating. This gives them vision they need to make a decision, per one of the most persuasive men in history, the late, great Jim Camp who was known for saying, ***"Vision drives decision"***.

Even The Bible reads…

Without Vision The People Perish!

You must *show* them the path.

Not merely tell them about it. Short story long: You can't overuse stories in both your marketing and the content you're creating. And especially when it comes to writing emails, I have a simple motto.

It's this:

When in doubt, tell a story!

Next up you'll gather what has been called the "raw material" for any sales message with…

Irresistible Bullets That Are Like An Itch That Your Readers Simply *Must* Scratch!

An old adage in copywriting is *it's all about the bullets*.

Here is where you are going to tease…in point form…all the goodies and benefits to be found "inside" your product and service. There is both an art and a science to this. Copywriters spend years studying to master this incredibly valuable skill. That's because one good bullet point (with enough curiosity, intrigue, fantasy…and belief in the right proportion) can be the "shot between the eyes" that gets a prospect to ante up and plunk down the moolah for your product or service – even if they'd never heard of you ten minutes ago!

For our purposes, there are really four main types of bullets most relative novices can pull off without too much difficulty:

1. Straight benefit

This is the most straightforward and easiest to write.

Basically, it tells of a lovely benefit your market will enjoy from using your lovely product or service, often expressed as "how to get [awesome, super-cool benefit here]". This can and must refer to your market research. What do they most fervently want? How can they "live the dream", as they say? Remember, marketers are genies. We make wishes come true. What deep, dark fantasies can you fulfill?

Here's one I wrote in the baseball niche:

- **The single most effective way to maximize any practice you do in a batting cage** (use this simple "mental cue" and your son will find himself reliably hitting more line drives over the in-field)

Note the "tack on" benefit in parentheses.

This is a common technique in copywriting. Describe a benefit, then use a parenthesis to lay out an additional benefit that expands on the first benefit. Sort of like a 1-2 punch.

2. Curiosity

Curiosity, almost more than any other emotion, can be the trigger for people to buy.

That's why it's worth it to get good at teasing the content in your offers. This works especially well with information products. If the promise matches your readers' desires it can become the itch they simply have to scratch – by buying your product, that is! Think of creative ways to hint at what it is without actually saying it. Hall-of-fame copywriters like Gary Halbert and Gary Bencivenga are good ones to study. They are/were monsters when it came to writing bullets. And theirs are positively *dripping* with curiosity.

Here's one of mine from the internet marketing niche:

✓ **A secret way to experience explosive profit growth starting today...without learning a single new marketing tactic!** (If you've ever felt intimidated at the thought of having to spend years figuring out how to launch your idea, getting this simple concept could change all of that instantly!) Page 36

Notice the contrasting ideas; *explosive profit growth/no new marketing*.

That's a disconnect that your brain needs to resolve. Ideally by purchasing the product! Use of contrast is a tried and true way to rev up the curiosity factor. This language, by the way, *if you've ever felt intimidated at the thought of having to spend years having to launch your idea* is taken verbatim from my market research. I'm holding up the mirror. Showing them they're understood, and therefore, in the right place.

More on how to get info like this in the next chapter

3. Tell 'em what not to do

Avoidance based copy can often be stronger than enticement.

That's because avoiding pain, failure or discomfort can often be a more powerful driver than the pursuit of gain. If you can hint at something your prospect could be currently doing that is hurting them in some way (and make it believable) that's hard to ignore. These bullets typically start with phrases like "the #1 thing you must never do" or "the 5 biggest mistakes most people make" and are ones to pepper in where possible.

Here's an example, again from an ad I wrote in the baseball niche:

- **3 common "bad bat angles" that destroy hitters' averages** (and the <u>exact</u> drills you need to correct them) 53:11...

This brings me to another point:

It's a great idea to balance benefits with some avoidance throughout your copy but especially in your bullets. Varying up the menu will add some spice and help keep interest high.

Ok, last but not least…

4. Proof

When it comes to sales copy remember this simple rule:

Proof is KING.

The only claim in marketing that matters is the one that you can prove.

The more you can infuse your copy with proof the better. The way this pans out when you're writing a bullet is a bit different since you are in effect not revealing the whole mechanism. In a nutshell what you want to do is reference sources that are credible to juice up that particular bullet's attraction and belief muscles.

Here's one I wrote:

- **A simple method (used by The Olympics and the world's top professional sports leagues) to draw viewers to your social media pages in droves! Page 74**

If you look carefully you'll see each of these examples contain an element of curiosity.

Together with belief and self-interest, these are the overarching emotions I'm trying to foment when I do write bullets. Proof-based bullets often begin with statements such as "a scientifically proven way to" include mention of a credible source such as "discovered by neuroscientists", or it could be something intriguing like "used by the great philosophers of Ancient Greece."

Anyway, that'll do her for now.

Yes, there are many more ways to do bullets effectively but they are beyond the scope of this book.

Use what you see here, and you won't go too far from the mark. Let's say you include 10, 15, 30 bullets on a page, try to rotate between each of the four above and this will give you enough variety to keep things fresh throughout. There's a rule:

What Is Fresh Gets Consumed!

What is stale gets discarded.

You don't want your sales copy to be discarded, do you?

Keep it fresh!

One more thing:

As a general rule, the higher your price-point, the more bullets you need. The idea is to build value in your product or service. The old-school direct response copywriters devoted a lot of real estate to the bullets. That's because you're never sure which one will put you over the edge. It's like having a dozen, to two dozen or three dozen at bats to finally knock one out of the park. Also, there's a compounding effect you get with trotting out a smorgasbord of bullets. It makes people go, "look how much is in this!" This is just another reason bullets can be hard for a prospect to ignore.

What I'll say is this:

If you're not uniquely skilled at writing bullets, you're always better off hiring a good copywriter…even if it's just to do a critique. The "secret sauce" that makes having lots and lots of bullets work is they must be interesting and well-written. Otherwise all you have is a lot of text. You can also make an attempt yourself by writing as many as you can come up with and going with the ones you feel are the strongest.

When it comes down to it I'd rather have fewer bullets on a page if that means they are higher-quality.

Alright, it's time to bring this doggy home.

Next is the part where you…

Close The Sale Like A Champ!

This is where you wrap up your sales message and ask for what you want.

Exciting times.

You'd be surprised how many websites or emails I review don't have a clear call to action. What are the next steps? Depending on the goal of your message this may be to register for your free webinar, book a free consultation, or buy your book or training program. I personally don't like to beat around the bush when it comes to closing.

You can use a short, punchy transition, something like:

> "Well, there's a taste of what you get in [name of your offer]. Here's the deal:"

Then you begin the close.

The close will recap the offer and tell them the price. If it's a special offer it will hopefully include some explanation as to why it's on offer, otherwise known as the "reason for the deal." Frankly, I don't think this gets enough attention. You need a good offer that your market wants. That's number one. But if you have plausible and believable scarcity that will almost certainly put you over the top in terms of the success of your offer. You want them to continue to believe all throughout. I can't emphasize this enough. If you've done your job, and you've built value, but you just kind of give away the farm without an explanation, you're going to set off some folks' BS meters.

Finally, while you want to be signaling a bit of urgency from the outset, in your close is where you'd also introduce any guarantees, bonuses or takeaways.

If There's No Deadline, It's Not Real!

That's just how human motivation works.

That goes double for this hyper-marketed age of too many choices and too much to do.

Our brains are actively looking for reasons to filter out actions that take up space on our already cluttered to-do lists. That's why you must be either specific with a deadline, as in "the price goes up at midnight" or use an implied deadline as in "order *today* to get the following special bonuses."

Straight Talk On Using Guarantees

If your product has a guarantee, such as a 30-day or 60-day or lifetime money back guarantee, in the close is also where you would explain it. You don't need a guarantee, but it's a good policy to have one. If cold prospects will be seeing your offer, I'd say it's almost mandatory.

I like having fun with guarantees. You can make them stand out with their own separate "box" on the page. And they're a great place to build further trust and cement the desire for the **outcome** your product or service promises. Remember, people buy results! It's not your product…it's what it can do for them.

Here's an example I wrote for the baseball niche:

> Simply put:
>
> I've been doing this a long time.
>
> And I'm 100% confident that if your son uses the connection ball with the drills I show you in the video, he'll hit the ball harder, hit with better launch angles, and almost instantly increase his batting average.
>
> That's why I'm willing to put my money where my mouth is.
>
> Use the connection ball and the video training for a full 60 days and if your son doesn't immediately feel more connected at his next at bat…if he's not hitting harder and farther after just a few practices…**if within two weeks of using these drills he's not the talk of the clubhouse with teammates coming to him, asking him for advice**…let us know and we'll refund your money on the spot.
>
> I'm not messing around with this either.
>
> I'm seen as a leader in the industry and I take my reputation VERY seriously.
>
> You'll either LOVE the results your son gets, or you don't pay.

What I tell business owners who bristle at this is:

Let's say you've got a customer who's angry or dissatisfied for whatever reason, you're probably going to give them their money back anyway. Might as well get credit for being a swell human being, and float it out there up front. Few will invoke it. (Assuming your product is good.) And often, this is a form of proof in that it demonstrates CONFIDENCE in what you're selling.

Also, I find it's best to tailor the guarantee to the offer.

In some cases, if what you're selling is highly valuable to your market, over-selling the guarantee comes across as suspicious and needy, and could *hurt* sales. Unfortunately, I can't tell you how to know when that's the case. You've got to *feel* it. Or at least think deeply about it.

Next up you're going to…

Drop In Bonuses That *Swell* The Value In Your Offer So Much, It'll Move Planets!

Bonuses are a great way to build even more value in what you're selling.

They can also be used to create urgency, per my example above. I like to think of a good bonus as anything rare (and ideally something with a demonstrable retail price) and that speaks to an emotional hot button you've uncovered in your buyers. A solid bonus can really put you over the top – even make the sale all on its own. These are easy to create.

We'll cover this topic in more detail later, but here's one idea:

Get someone to interview you for 30-60 minutes sharing secrets you know your readers are interested in. Then, offer the transcript or audio as a bonus.

Well, there you have it.

It's brief, as outlines go.

But following the steps above on your landing page BEFORE you reach out to anyone with the offer via email can mean the difference between success and failure.

Next up, my secrets for creating high-converting lead magnets that attract new subscribers to your list in droves and pre-qualify prospects so only your best potential customers contact you.

Chapter 2

The Art Of The Lead Magnet

"A lot of times, people don't know what they want until you show them."

–Steve Jobs

Next up on our journey…

If you'd like to easily attract new leads who are 80% sold on your product or service before they ever talk to you…and do it without a complicated "maze" of autoresponder sequences (these are email sequences automatically delivered by a CRM or email automation software such a Aweber or MailChimp)…then this chapter will give you the 4-1-1 on exactly how I do this for my clients.

The lead magnet is something that is talked about a fair bit but I'm going to reveal my unique take on it.

Basically….

Your Lead Magnet Is Bait.

It helps you "hook" your ideal customers.

It's a tool for getting folks to raise their hands (as in give you an email address or other contact info) and step out from lurking in the shadows as a "suspect" into the broad daylight of becoming a "prospect" who has – at the very least – a *demonstrated* interest in what you have to offer. And via your lead magnet you also have an opportunity to begin the process of educating your customer, per the Steve Jobs quote I opened this chapter with.

Your magnet could be almost anything that has perceived value to your market…

...A video tutorial, a quiz that reveals something useful, a webinar, a whitepaper, a PDF or an e-book.

Some people would say it doesn't matter as long as it appears valuable enough to give away contact info. Others still would say the PDF is dead. That people hate them. They don't read them. I would disagree with those people. My preference...and you can call me old fashioned...is still to do a free report.

Tell you why in a sec.

I am currently doing this in over two dozen niches and they DO convert. And, in my experience the people who read them tend to be better customers; more compliant, respectful, and overall just more serious. My preference is to position your lead magnet as a "consumer awareness guide".

Next, you're going to call out important facts about your industry.

For instance, one chiropractor I work with had developed a very accurate health test. So I referenced the fact that *x-rays produce 50% false positives* (this is true by the way – doctors will admit it). The idea is to highlight important facts about your industry, product, or service your customers should care about and...

Tell Them What To Look For!

In so doing, you'll lay out the *buying criteria*.

Not only that, but your clever little self is going to demonstrate how your product or service meets those criteria so ably that...by the end of the day...you'll be the OBVIOUS choice. Result? You've told them what to look for. You've shown them how your product ticks all those boxes. And this is important – in a *non-needy* way. I can't overstate how powerful this is. You're essentially going, "whether you buy from me or not, here's what you want to do" and it's the subtext that's leaving a trail of bread crumbs that leads right back to, you guessed it...YOU.

When you follow this very specific format, you'll be providing your prospect a document that to its core is a sales letter, <u>but it feels like content</u>. There's no hype or urgency needed. You're just walking them through the process which has but one inevitable conclusion: buying from you!

Ok, without further ado...

Here it is in 5 easy steps:

1. Headline

This can be as simple as repeating your guide's title (maybe preceded by a short statement about who it's for). Personally, I like to do a true direct-response headline here. I just think it captures attention, which is what I want. I want them to read the whole thing as soon as they download it.

You can refer to the previous chapter for my thoughts on writing an effective headline.

2. Lead Paragraph

This is a brief paragraph to introduce your content. Approach this as "why they should care" or "what you'll get out of reading this guide". Your goal is to lock in their attention and get them to keep reading. Check out the previous chapter for my best practices on this one.

3. Your 5 Facts

This is where you spell out your five facts or buying criteria.

Keep each one short and to the point.

Maybe 1-3 paragraphs each.

How do you come up with these? That will be a product of your research. In general, what you're looking for are facts about your industry or your service or product they may not know but that's relevant to their desires. Statistics are great for this. Think of what you would say if you had less than a minute to talk to a stadium full of people. How would you quickly interest the greatest number of potential customers possible?

We'll circle back to this idea in Chapter 4 and I'll share a few different examples of what I mean.

4. Close

Tell them very simply that this concludes the guide.

Recap what to look out for. Then tell them if they want **x** (x being whatever benefit(s) your product or service amply provides) then do this next…and walk them through the next steps of getting involved with you. You can put an offer or not. That's optional.

5. Testimonial(s)

This one is optional as well.

I like to include one to several testimonials. If you've been paying attention, you'll realize this looks suspiciously like the format for a sales letter. Very good. Full points. There is a basic underlying reason for this: it's just a good flow that's proven to work for a persuasive letter, report, or guide.

Listen, if it ain't broke…don't fix it.

No point reinventing the wheel.

Rome wasn't built in a day.

[Insert other cliché here.]

You get the drift.

At the end of this book you can read a sample guide I created for my industry. There you'll see the five steps above in action. It's one you can easily model to create your own.

Onwards.

Next we get into the most fun part of any project: the research!

Andale!

Chapter 3

The Customer Prototype

"Seek first to understand, then to be understood."
–Habit #5 from Dr. Stephen Covey's *7 Habits Of Highly Effective People*

Meaty chapter this one.

Or, lots of plant-based protein if you're vegetarian. Just lots of protein in general. It'll be a full meal you'll want to digest slowly. Not because of its length.

Instead because…

With Nothing Else Than This One Simple Exercise You Can Almost "Fail Proof" Your Emails!

This is the first exercise I do with any new email client.

Without exception I've been told it was one of the most valuable things they've ever done. Problems like low open rates, low engagement, low clickthrough rates, low sales, high unsubscribes, not knowing what to write about, not knowing what to say to generate interest in your offers, or getting lots of *resistance* to your offers…

ALL come from not having a simple tool like the customer prototype I recommend you create.

What is it?

Think of it as a cheat sheet.

Here's why:

It's Everything You Need To Know About Your Best Customer...In A Single Page.

And more.

I'll explain in a minute.

First, here's what you want to know:

Who are they (age range, demographic, education, income)? Where do they live? What sort of places do they go? What kind of books or TV shows do they consume? What other influences have their attention? What sort of things do they care about? What are their biggest fears, hopes, frustrations? Who are their enemies? Who are their heroes? What do they aspire to in the future and what are the main sticking points or objections they could have that might stop them buying from you?

Having it all mapped out ahead of time will be a boon when it comes to communicating and converting people. It's likely that you deal with a range of customers. There will be some variables that obviously don't apply to all of them. With the customer prototype, what we're really trying to do is narrow in on our best guess about all of this stuff...as far as it concerns our *ideal* customer.

First, give your prototype the name of a person.

This serves as a **customer avatar**.

From now on, whenever you write or prepare any marketing, be it a sales letter or an email, you are writing specifically to THAT person. This makes it a lot easier to decide what to say. You see that person in your mind's eye and you're simply going to have a dialogue (one-sided though it may be).

Stuck for what content to create? Let's go to the customer prototype. Want to make sure you're hitting the right "high notes" and not missing any potential concerns that might put the brakes on the sale? The prototype. All the answers are there, forever more. You can see how having a tool like this streamlines everything and makes it simpler, easier, and faster to come up with persuasive communication that makes your market feel understood.

That's when you get comments like…

"It Feels Like You're Writing To Me."

In case you missed it…that's a *good* thing.

Real good, in fact.

Alright, now that we've covered what the customer prototype is and why you want one, let's take a look at where you'll find the answers to all of the above so you can create this sucker.

Chapter 4

Researching Your Market

"Our main business is not to see what lies dimly at a distance, but to do what lies clearly at hand." – Robert Carlyle

Let's talk market research.

As you prepare to write to your subscriber list your goal is to know as much as possible about what's going on with your prospect. When you're able to effectively inhabit their world, you can do what Robert Collier said and "enter the conversation already occurring in the prospect's mind".

First, here's your check up from the neck up:

In terms of your approach, you want to get to the point where you're able to write a page in their diary better than they can. That's the attitude I would take. And if you do, that gives you immense power in knowing how to persuade your reader and motivate them to take action. But it also makes writing your emails (and any form of promotion) very, very easy because you already have all the answers. You're not "winging it", so to speak. You're not making things up. You're not shooting from the hip.

It's not like you don't know where to start…

You Start With *Them.*

Top A-list copywriter Doug D'Anna says:

> *Don't build a bridge from your product to your market.*
> *Build a bridge from your market to your product.*

Let me share a story to illustrate this.

I started with a client a while back and as happens quite often, they were pretty keen and wanted to see what kind of content I was coming up with, almost right away. What I explained to the client was that my process was to do research first and really understand the market that I'm writing to, otherwise I'm not able to be effective as your copywriter.

So I said:

"What you need to understand is *I don't actually write anything.*"

Here's what I mean by that.

I asked him, "You do a consultative sales process, correct?" He said yes. "Well, in a consultative sale, think about what you're doing; you are asking your prospect a lot of questions to help them clarify what their problem is…then you're *holding up the mirror* so they can see it even more clearly. Essentially, that's how you're able to create within them the desire and the urgency to take advantage of your solution to that particular problem. It's putting the problem in front of them in definite and certain terms. It's defining it, making it real, and making it bigger. It's making it emotional so they feel like they have to get rid of the problem. In effect, that's what you're doing, yes?"

He agreed.

"Copywriting is salesmanship in print," I explained.

The goal is the same.

The disadvantage you have is that copywriting as a sales medium is much harder. In a consultation, you're able to ask questions and dig out the information you need. When you send someone a letter or they arrive on your sales page online, you can do quizzes and that sort of thing, but for the most part the letter is pre-written. So you really want to get into the mindset of knowing what the answers to those questions are beforehand.

So when I say to the client, "I don't write anything," that's the reality.

In fact, what I do instead is…

An Almost *Unreasonable* Amount of Research!

It may not sound sexy.

But oh boy if you can learn to get excited about this, it will change everything.

I do a lot of research. I get to know my market, their verbiage, their way of seeing things and their way of thinking. Then, I just reflect it back to them. Then the words that I'm using are not my words or the client's words that I'm projecting on them. They are the market's own words. How they talk, how they think, how they describe things, how they describe their problems, how they describe your product.

This is important because really, one wrong word, or an expression that they don't quite understand, or you are projecting on them your beliefs or your value system, it's going to cost you sales. Let's say I'm writing to an older crowd. I'm going to think twice about using a colloquialism like "That's how I roll." Just off the top of my head. Is there a chance some of this crowd knows what that expression means? Of course. Do most of them? Probably not. Why would you take that risk? If it's going to go over their heads, if they're not going to understand it, they're going to immediately start to lose interest in your copy, and that's obviously not what you want.

When I say you should be able to write a page in their diary what I mean is, really, the more you know the better. Sometimes it's hard to answer some of these questions as precisely as I would like to, but the more you know, the easier it will be to write to them because the answers of what to say are always in your market.

Let me give you an example with my personal training business I had for years.

After a while, I was so knowledgeable about my clients that...

I Could Write A Page In Their Diary Better Than They Could!

For fun, I did this exercise once.

I sent an email to my list with the subject line *"I stole her diary."*

In the email I "impersonated" a generic woman that could have been my client and wrote what I think she thinks, and what she'd feel and write in her diary. You wouldn't believe the responses I got. Several were along the lines of "Holy cow, this *is* me." When you start to do email well, you'll get responses like that too. You'll hear things like, "Wow, I really feel like this was written to me."

And that's a great sign.

The "unfair" advantage is, having done that business for so many years, I'd had hundreds of sales consultations, thousands of conversations with clients, and these allowed me to interact with my market directly. It was also years of replies to my emails. There was almost no way for me to go wrong with that kind of education and insider's knowledge about my customers. I knew them so well. I knew what their struggles were. *That's* what I want for you.

The challenge is most businesses don't have that level of interaction with their customers.

Personal training is indeed very *personal,* and therefore, it lends itself to knowing a lot about your clients. That's not to say other business owners couldn't try to know all this stuff about their customers and clients because there really is power in knowing it. And I think sometimes, business owners do drop the ball by not having more personal conversations and getting into these scenarios in depth with the clients that they serve.

What kind of things should you know about your market?

Demographics certainly.

Things like age, gender, income and where they live are all pretty important. How educated they are because that will inform your choices about words and language. Are they religious or spiritual? What sorts of things do they care about? What does their typical week look like, what does their typical day look like? What do they do on weekends? What are some of their favorite pastimes? Who do they follow on social media, who do they read, what sorts of movies do they watch?

You may not be able to drill down to specifics on that, but my experience is in most businesses, there are generalities. And if you're open and truly looking for them, you will find them. The more educated guesses you can make, the better position you'll be in to market to and sell your best prospects. I mean your best prospects. Think about your clients or customers that are your favorite customers and are the highest profit to you, the easiest to deal with, your ideal customer, and then form your assumptions based on them. Get to know them because really, you want a bunch more of exactly that type of person.

If they make such great clients for you guess who else will…

Other People That Are Like Them… And __Think__ Like Them!

Makes sense, doesn't it?

Next we get into *psychographics*.

Now, I've covered this already a little bit in the customer prototype. The psychographics are things like fears, frustrations, dreams, and aspirations. What do they want, what is it they're trying to avoid, what are their pains and problems? If you can talk to people who have bought from you before and ask deep probing questions, see if you can get to what Gary Halbert called their ***core buying desire***, which is the main reason that they bought from you in the first place. If you're able to know the main thing that causes them to buy, and the main outcome they want, and if you lead with that, you're in a very strong position to know which high notes to hit in any format.

You want to know what bugs them, too. What problems do they currently have? List them out. What are their insecurities, what keeps them up at night, what causes them stress? What mistakes are they making currently that are preventing them from having this number one outcome that you've recognized that they want?

That last one can be fodder for a list email that outlines multiple mistakes. Also, each mistake can be its own email. People will read that type of email all day. If it's about a possible mistake that they're making *currently* that is holding them back from something they want, that's definitely something very captivating that is hard to ignore and…

This Makes Your <u>Emails</u> Almost Impossible To Ignore.

This is something you want.

That's **if** you want sales, more customer loyalty, and engagement in general.

PRO TIP: one thing I insist on with my clients (and this is something that you should do if you are doing any form of regular email) is *read responses and keep a file where you save responses*. Just have a document saved on your desktop and as interesting replies come in, copy and paste them into the doc.

There is no end of great information in the responses to emails that you send to your list. I mean relevant responses of course, i.e. ones that have to do with the content, or are stories about them. Using this method, you can build up your own private swipe file of the kinds of expressions and the kinds of words your customers are using when describing their problem or your service or product.

Any time you're stuck for content (and even if you're not stuck) go back and reread that file.

Good tip.

Use it.

Next, here's the quickie version of how you're going to answer all these questions about your market we've been asking. There are four main things you want to concern yourself with. You could do this in a single afternoon and you'd be miles ahead of your nearest competitor in terms of what you know about your customers.

The #1 thing that not enough business owners do, is just to…

Interact With People In Your Market.

That's the easiest and best way to do it.

Whether it's via the responses they send to your emails, or you can simply go and talk to your customers. Or, if you don't have customers or buyers yet, you talk to people that are in your prospective market, and you ask them a bunch of questions (and you record it if you get permission) and take notes. You build up a file on all this research that you're collecting with quotes in it, and that kind of thing. Doing this, you'll quickly get a strong sense for how they talk and what sort of wording to use on things. You'll also get glimpses into what they think about and feel about certain things.

This can also be done by interviewing your clients.

(Again record everything and transcribe. This is GOLD. You'll have dozens of pages replete with your customers talking about their problems, and here's the kicker, *in their own words*.)

Ok, step two.

Haunt message boards or Facebook groups where your market hangs out. There you'll discover reams of high-quality information about your prospect. You can read long threads and see what they're talking about, what they're bitching about, what they hate, and what are the central themes they discuss.

Three, and this is a favorite of mine.

I've gotten tons of great market insights from doing this.

It's going on **Amazon** and reading the reviews for books related to what you're selling.

Once I was asked to critique a sales page in the college admissions industry. This particular company was helping parents with the application and admissions process to get their kids into college. I wanted to provide some samples of how I would sell the service, and in the process I hammered out a few bullets. Keep in mind, *I hadn't seen what's in the service at this point.* The bullets mostly came from Amazon comments, and from my other research.

Normally, when I create bullets, I have the product. I read or watch it and I highlight anything interesting, and those notes form the basis for my bullets. But you really don't even need to do that. Just by reading the Amazon reviews about books related to college admissions, I uncovered tons of gold.

You'll find some people just leave a, "Great book!" Or something like that. That's not helpful. But if you go look at the ones who leave a long review, oftentimes they'll go on a tangent about what was the specific problem or pain that they had before they got the book, as justification for buying it or how it helped (or didn't help). That's where you'll really dig out the pearls.

Last but not least:

Research Important Facts About Your Industry Or Marketplace.

Here's the type of fact you're looking for.

It's something that could be used as a "catch all". What I mean by that is you want facts that will be interesting to a broad audience as a way of bringing them on board. The best analogy I've heard for this is to call it a *stadium pitch*, as I mentioned in Chapter 2. If you had to be in front of a crowd of 50,000 and you had one minute to attract their interest in your product, what would you say? A great way is to lead with an interesting stat that will awaken curiosity for what you've got.

One example: I was doing some writing for the physiotherapy market. I came across this stat the business owner did not know about. According to research, 70% of people who went to physio as a first intervention for back pain found that they had a positive outcome. That right there is a great vote for *if I have back pain, I should be interested in physio*; whereas prior to hearing that, it may not have been on their radar.

See how this works?

Another one was for a tech startup targeting the independent health provider market such as chiropractors, physicians, nurses, naturopathic doctors, massage therapists, personal trainers, etc. We were trying to interest them in starting their own "mobile care" practice – which is essentially offering home visits – by highlighting the revenue opportunity. Well, there's a huge shift happening, away from clinical care, towards home care. And there had been a paper published by *Grand View Research* stating that the home healthcare industry would reach $556B by 2026. That's a massive number and it gets attention. Also, it just sort of paints with broad strokes a picture of why anybody would be interested in starting a home care business.

There you have it.

It's the cribs notes version of market research. I recommend you book off an afternoon and work your way through these steps, taking your time, and making a big pile of notes. You'll be fascinated as you get into it what you can find. It truly is one of the most intriguing and rewarding parts of the process. And it's one I've come to absolutely love. You'll find hooks and ways to persuade and sell you wouldn't have thought of otherwise. As I said to one client, "Patience, I'm looking for something. I'll know what it is when I find it!"

Chapter 5

Writing Emails That Convert

"Successful salesmen are rarely good speech makers. They have few oratorical graces. They are plain and sincere men who know their customers and know their lines. So it is in ad writing."

–Advertising legend Claude Hopkins in *Scientific Advertising*

Next up, here are seven email types that I believe anyone in any industry can use to start making a lot more sales as of today.

If you currently market yourself with email, this could be one of the most valuable things you lay your ambitious eyes upon all year. In this chapter, I'm going to pull back the curtains and reveal a lot about copywriting and persuasion in general, as well as about my own approach to writing emails.

First, a quick story:

Once upon a time a subscriber forwarded me an email of a very well-known fitness guy which was a clear rip off of one of my emails. I'm not going to name names. Not sure where this famous marketer saw my content, maybe he was on my list using an email address that doesn't identify him. But the point is my subscriber was not impressed. Now at the time I was flattered more than anything that such a big name even cared enough about my stuff to rip it off, so I didn't pursue the issue.

But I could have.

The point is carelessly swiping is not only unproductive, but can be a liability as well. That's not what you should do with the examples below. What I'd like you to do instead is to get the concepts that I'm explaining here and *model* I'm doing for your business. It's not that difficult. I've pulled emails from different niches so that you can see that this works across the board in all industries. And you can get a flavor for how I've tweaked them for the specific industry that I'm in.

All right, first email.

EMAIL TYPE #1: The Story Email

I have a very simple motto…

When in doubt, tell a story!

You almost can't go wrong telling stories and lots of stories in your marketing in general, but in emails specifically. That's my default if I'm stuck for content. They are naturally engaging and everybody can tell a story.

For this particular email the client was a chiropractor who owns a multi-disciplinary health clinic. Also, we're promoting a half-price massage. As we'll find out a bit later, your offers are very important when it comes to how well your emails convert. And as it happens, a half-price massage is a very good offer and I've yet to see it not convert in almost any niche.

Let's take a look:

SUBJECT: The superpower we all possess but seldom use

My five year old son says he's Spiderman today.

True story.

I came down for breakfast, and there he was: fully decked out in his Spiderman gear, eating a bowl of cornflakes.

He just woke up and decided that's who he wants to be.

"Sounds great, Spidey, don't forget your superhero's lunch, all that fighting crime builds up an appetite," his Mom chimed in.

And I thought, "how cool is that??"

As adults, we forget we have that ability too.

I'm not suggesting you put on a cape to go the office...

(Although you could.)

But what if you woke up and anointed yourself the superhero in your own life, just for today?

How would you do things differently?

What could you accomplish?

Good one to chew on.

Of course, all of this is a heck of a lot easier to pull off when you feel good...you know, when you've got that sense of calm, deep down in your bones? When you feel like you can take on all comers, and you brush stress off your shoulders like so much lint?

If it's been a while since you've felt that way, check out today's special offer of **50% off your next massage** here at the clinic:

[Link]

You deserve it.

While I can't guarantee you'll be leaping tall buildings in a single bound, I do know you'll have a better day than if you *don't* get a massage.

Maybe even kick some bad-guy butt...

Yours In Great Health,

Dr. Nick

Let's look at this subject line first.

> *"The superpower we all possess but seldom use."*

That right there is a curiosity-based subject line. "We all have a superpower we don't use?" That's what your reader is thinking. You really can't do too much curiosity in your openers. You'll see that theme throughout this book. Curiosity is a powerful hook. The more you can make you subject headings the "itch" they simply have to scratch, the better.

For a little background, this was one of my first clients when I got into this business, and he was *my* chiropractor. He was cracking my back one day, as chiropractors do, and told me this story, which I embellished a little and converted it to an email. It turned out that they liked what I'd done, and that was how I basically acquired him as a client.

Note:

We All Tell Stories Like This Every Day.

The trick is to have your antenna up.

Pay attention to the stories you tell. Write them down. You can repurpose them later.

Here's how I want you to think about this: the most highly converting stories that I've ever used in any niche are ones that give people an *experience* when they read it. You're trying to create an emotion. If it's an emotion that you can tie to your product, you're miles ahead of the game in terms of persuading someone to take advantage of your offer. You're creating a state in your reader that fuels their desire. So when you write a story, think first of all about what your offer is and what emotion you want to evoke. That's ultimately going to spur them to take action. Here I'm creating that feeling of "Aaaah" and feeling great, of having power and confidence and strutting down the street.

You can see how the story does this.

Alright, enough about that.

Example #2:

EMAIL TYPE #2: The "Show, Don't Tell" Email

This is the second type of email that I've found almost always converts.

I call this the "show, don't tell" email. And the concept is you're *demonstrating* what you do or what your product or service does for people. If it's an email about a testimonial, that's a really easy way to do it. You just more or less plug in the testimonial from your customer or client, and then you write a few little short comments underneath, and that'll work just fine for doing this particular type of email. Be forewarned…

This Is Uniquely Powerful!

It must be used only with the best of intentions.

I wrote this email for a niche I was doing at one point, Google AdWords campaigns for attorneys:

Subject: Google Rep Vs. The Muscle: The Smackdown

For your viewing pleasure today...

The results from a little experiment I did to amuse myself.

See I was contacted by a Google Adwords rep offering to "improve" a campaign I'm running in one of the niches I serve.

And while that strikes me as somewhat like giving the inmates the keys to the asylum, I thought, let's see what she does.

I didn't tell her I'm an Adwords consultant.

Here's what happened:

First, she didn't ask a single question about what my goals are.

She just talked over me the whole time.

Then she offered to build out a new campaign for me.

So I let her.

Are you ready for it?

Drum roll please...

Here are **seven days** (which is as long as I would permit this bloodbath to continue) of her campaign vs. seven days of the campaign I'd already built:

Google rep
28 Clicks
2.5% Clickthrough Rate
$12.19 Average Cost Per Click
Total cost $352.95
0 Conversions

Me (The Muscle)
57 Clicks
3.58% Clickthrough Rate
$4.13 Average Cost Per Click
Total cost $235.59
3 Conversions

(Conversions are leads.)

Yup, it's definitive.

That's a smackdown.

I gave her the courtesy of my finishing move...the back-twisting double-somersaulting Adwords ninja.

And this is now officially the most expensive email I've ever produced as it cost me $352.95 to bring you this little insight.

She tried to convince me that our interests were aligned.

In theory, they are. If I'm making money from my ads, I'll keep spending on them.

But as you know very well Counselor, theory and practice are two different things.

Don't buy the charm offensive.

Instead, buy results:

http://legalmarketingmuscle.com/freeconsult/

Let The Muscle lay the smackdown on your competition too.

Happy Winning,

Conor Kelly
The Muscle @Legal Marketing Muscle

Subject line:

"Google rep vs. the muscle: the smackdown"

Right off the bat, I have to tell you that this subject line got a very high open rate.

My hunch is two things: one, it's just a weird subject line. It's not a typical subject line that you would get. Anything you can do to make your subject lines weird in some way, it makes them stand out. And second, "Google rep versus the muscle" implies some sort of story, which again is inherently interesting to people.

Always keep in mind, people will *say* they want to be informed, but they'd rather be entertained. Who gets paid more in our society, teachers or entertainers? The best way to do all of this, any type of marketing, whether it's public speaking or building your website, email, whatever, is to…

Combine Content With Promotion!

This email, as you can see, does content with promotion.

And it adds a little bit of fun too, with expressions like "for your viewing pleasure today."

It's that splash of personality.

Using words like "bloodbath" too, very colorful. Any time you can add color and drama and visual to your writing or to your emails or any form of copy, it's very powerful. Again: *I gave her the courtesy of my finishing move, the back-twisting, double-somersaulting AdWords ninja.* You can see I'm having fun with this. Also, depending on your market, lingo and language that reflects words familiar to them is very useful to put in email too. You see here I add "As you know very well, Counselor."

Remember, I'm speaking to attorneys.

This could actually have been better if I added a little bit more urgency to it. For example, *I'm only taking on one new client this month.* As it happened I didn't need it. I got a client out of this email, so that's another testament to how powerful this type of email can be. If you're demonstrating your value with your stories, you can quickly acquire sales even without some of the other action drivers or psychological triggers that you would typically need. It's the demonstration that does most of the heavy lifting. That, in and of itself, creates desire for your product or service.

Hence, "show, don't tell."

Okay, next email type.

EMAIL TYPE #3: The Confessional Email

The confessional is almost without exception the first broadcast message or first email in an auto-responder series for any new client. Why? It's a shot between the eyes and for most, a sudden and dramatic change in tone. It wakes their audience up. The confessional email does two things. One, it's very personal and revealing and it connects you to the reader.

As the saying goes…

Disclosure Is Disarming.

Disclose a little bit about yourself when it makes sense to do so.

It immediately lets people in. And what's more…it lets their guard down. Also, note that what I'm doing subtly here, that I've done in other types of emails in other formats, is…

Talking About Problems!

First, you should know what your market's problems are.

The kind of problems you spell out in a confessional are those that your market has, and that you either share with your market sometimes (because you're admitting you're not perfect), or *was* a problem that you've had in the past. When you talk about someone's problems, you almost can't lose their attention. Their problems are urgent for them right now. Parris Lampropoulos, a great copywriter still working today, once said that you want to be *very specific about the problem* but…

Be Vague About The Solution.

So drill down deep.

Get as specific about the problem as you can in your emails, and just offer a little bit of the solution so that they have to contact you to get the full fix. All right, let's get into this next email here:

SUBJECT: PRIVATE PHOTO: How to feel beautiful, right now

Hi Conor,

Why am I showing you this photo of me without makeup?

[photo]

I've never shared this before...

But I wasn't always super confident about my looks.

In fact, there was a time when I even considered myself unattractive.

The truth is I never was. That's just something you tell yourself when you're not honoring who you are....when you're not owning the power of that wonderful, complicated, sexy creature that is YOU, my dear.

Ever have days when you feel like that?

Maybe it's been a while since a mysterious, handsome stranger shot you a lingering glance. Or maybe you've just been too busy doing that woman thing you do where you look after everybody else, but don't make time for yourself.

But here's the thing: feeling beautiful is a function of LOVING yourself. Because when you're in the emotion of loving and appreciating all that you are, you radiate with a warmth and charm that gives others around you permission to be that way too.

That quality is beyond attractive.

It's IRRESISTIBLE.

How do you love yourself on those less-than-perfect days?

The same way you love anybody else...

With your actions.

So tell me: what 3 things will you do today, to show love to yourself and make yourself feel beautiful?

Good one to think about.

Alright, that's all for today.

I'm going to take my dogs for a walk. Then, it'll be time for 'Mom' to have a little pampering of her own.

Remember, show yourself some love today, girl.

You deserve it.

Ana

P.S. **How do we consistently deliver "fitness model" physiques** to thousands of Toronto women just like you? One word: *personalization*. You have your own unique body type and challenges. We are the women's fitness experts with the answers you need:

=>Click here to view our personal training programs while spots last.

This email had one of the highest open rates on any subject line I've ever done.

Here's why. First:

"How to feel beautiful right now"

Instant benefit.

And it's a benefit this market wants. There's an immediate payoff to opening this email. That's what we're telling them. Second, the "dirty trick" that's giving us a little stealth persuasion is this expression right here: PRIVATE PHOTO. People are voyeurs. Anytime you can add in the word *private* or *personal* or *for your eyes only* or *exclusive* or *do not share*, those emails will typically get a much higher open rate. Personally, I don't like to use them very often. I consider it more of a "nuclear" option, but nevertheless it's there. I submit that to you.

You can use it when you want to get your emails opened.

Getting into the body of this email now, a lot of the women that are reading are really connecting with it. The client is someone who is out there on Instagram as a fitness model and has lots of modeling pictures. She's built her brand around being beautiful. So for her to come out and admit "I didn't always feel beautiful", "I don't always feel attractive", there's a lot of power and wow factor in that for her audience. You can kind of see the contrast I'm using. The confessional is "like you, I don't always feel beautiful." And we're going a little bit into the pain of that. And then we hint at the fantasy of the other side, the handsome stranger shooting you a lingering glance, or when you *do* feel beautiful, what can happen.

Also, this little statement at the end, "I'm going to take my dogs for a walk and then have a little pampering," that's what we call a *live look-in*. People love those little look-ins to your life and what you're doing. It can be as simple as two lines that say, "Hey, here's what I'm up to today." If you're in front of them with any consistency, it helps build a relationship with your list.

I kind of went soft a bit on this email, because I actually wound up putting the call to action down in the P.S. And I understand why I did that. The email gave me such a good feeling that, as we got down to the end, it didn't feel genuine to disrupt that flow by putting in a call to action. But looking back on it, I could have done that too, e.g. *what are the three things you'll do today? One of them could be booking your free personal training consultation. You've got nothing to lose. There's absolutely no obligation.*

This is another point too.

A lot of the small businesses that I work with, the call to action is going be "Reply to this email" or "Call the office to make an appointment." In cases where you're actually having them click away to a sales page or an opt-in page to get them to take advantage of a free consultation or whatever the offer is, what's really important is *what's on the page* you're getting them to click through to.

This harkens back to Chapter 1 which was all about sales pages.

At the risk of sounding repetitive, you can have the greatest emails and you can do all this stuff to the T, but if you're not sending them to a high converting landing page, sales page, or sales letter, you are not going to get the results from your email program that you'd like. That's just a fact. (And that's something that I can help you with. Go to www.ConorKelly.com and sign up for my free email tips to learn more).

Again:

The real advantage of showing you these high-converting email types is that this is not only the key to being able to email your list more frequently, but it lets you…

Sell In Every Email!

And *still* have people thank you for it.

They know you're promoting to them but still feel like you've shared something of great value. That's the magic of using these particular email types; they will get you that kind of response. You'll have people write back to you and comment something or tell you how much they enjoyed it, while at the same time positively buying from you at a very high rate, because the way this all works, what holds it together is you're making them *feel* a certain way.

You're giving them an emotional response.

You're creating a state that leads them in a direction towards wanting to purchase or motivates them to take action in some way. Whatever your call of action happens to be.

Okay, that's enough about that. Let's forge ahead.

Email type number four:

EMAIL TYPE #4: The List Email

This is a very common email type.

3 Things everybody should know about X.

4 Ways to do Y.

7 Unhealthy "health foods".

You've seen this over and over again. The reason this works very well is because, among other things, a number is specific. People like lists. They're easily digested. And the specificity of the number is hard to resist. It's attractive and curiosity-provoking as it suggests content. And for people who like to scan, they just want to know what the things are, especially if it speaks to a pain point or something your prospect considers urgent to them. Just a few reasons why lists are…

One Of The Best Forms Of "Click Bait"!

You've likely been seduced by this at some point.

It could be an image or a "suggested" YouTube video with the headline *10 celebrities who lost it in interviews* or something silly like that. This is typically how click bait disguises her tempting ways. So this is a proven technique and it's used across the board in many mediums and formats.

All right, so let's take a look at this particular email:

Subject: 3 Biggest Success Blocks (Avoid These)

Confession time:

I wasn't always super confident, a good speaker, or successful in real estate.

Just the opposite… I made ALL the mistakes.

If you pay attention to this list, it'll help you avoid some of the struggles I went through, and open you up to all the success I know is possible for you.

Here we go with the 3 biggest success blocks:

1. Self-image. The story you have about WHO you are is always a self-fulfilling prophecy. It sets the limits of what you can achieve. That's because you can't act in a way that contradicts your self-image. Until you learn to see yourself as the type of person that attracts success, you'll always live down to your expectations, whether you're aware of them or not.

2. Pauper's mindset. I grew up poor. When 'not enough' has been a part of your life for a long time, your filter (the way you view the world) is one of scarcity. This 'limited pie' thinking says there's only so much to go around, and you should never have more than your fair share (or someone else's wealth is the reason you have less). If you believe that your access to money is limited IN ANY WAY, it's like standing on a garden hose...

Your abundance can't flow to you.

3. NOT taking action. Procrastination has killed more good ideas than laziness and bad luck combined. The only way to accomplish anything is to get started. Know anyone who's done it differently? Unless you're moving ahead, you won't get the feedback you need to correct course on your path, and make your dreams manifest.

Trouble is, these three are often "under the radar".

Only by paying attention to your thoughts and feelings (and your RESULTS, btw...life is your mirror), can you catch yourself in the act.

Then, it's about being ruthless at reprogramming your subconscious.

There's no such thing as too many books, audios, or seminars! I STILL invest thousands each year in my education. In fact, I became a hypnotist so I could put myself in a trance, and plant the beliefs I want at the deepest levels of my mind.

That's why, THIS WEEK ONLY, I'm giving you the chance to grab your copy of my *Trance For Your Success* audios at 80% off.

All of my most dedicated students use this:

=>Click here to remove the biggest blocks to your success.

Use promo code power1.

It's exactly how it sounds: I gently put you into a trance, and rewire your brain to be laser-focused on the success, love, and abundance you deserve.

Don't miss it!

Anyway, it's back to work for me.

I'm rehabbing a bathroom.

I'll send you some before and after pics when I'm done!

To Your Power,

[signature]

Right off the bat, if you can do lists of mistakes or avoidance based lists, these are really my favorite type of list to do because they speak to what they might currently be doing that is holding them back in some way. This gets attention and is also interesting.

You can see the subject line, *3 Biggest Success Blocks (Avoid These)* is very strong and it builds a ton of curiosity. It uses the number for specificity and it's avoidance based. I even say "avoid these". Just in case there was any doubt.

Getting right into the email, you see that first little statement right there? *Confession time*. I like to do this in a lot of my emails and it's something I learned from the great Ben Settle. It's to start with a short punchy statement as the first line. The reason is it just draws people into reading in an easy way. It could be two words, three words, or a sentence that fits on one line.

I wouldn't suggest you do that exactly the same way every time. Sometimes the opener is a paragraph, but many times I'll just do this short sentence.

Also, those two words are compelling.

People love confessions. They're juicy.

This also happens to be a trust trigger. This next paragraph is also significant:

> **If you pay attention to this list**, it'll help you avoid some of the struggles I went through, and open you up to all the success I know is possible for you.

Again, I don't do this every single time, but what I am doing here is *framing* the content.

This tells the reader what's in it for them, and what they can expect if they read it. It gets them wanting to read the whole thing. The client is a speaker who is a success trainer. He focuses on success training, personal development and success training for real estate, specifically. And one way he's unique among personal development gurus is that he's also a master hypnotist. If you go to see him speak, he will sometimes do a hypnotist show as part of his speech or at another time during the event. Very cool. Thus, part of his *shtick*, if you will, is being able to put you into a hypnotic trance and help reprogram your brain at that subconscious level, and it's a great idea. I mean, who wouldn't want that. We'd all love for someone to just come along and either wave a magic wand or hypnotize us into all of a sudden being the person that we want to be; the uber-confident, successful, attractive person we all fantasize about becoming.

Notice success block # 3: *not taking action.* I'm challenging them with this copy. And I'm lifting them up. This is a higher level conversation; one that's empowering.

Key point about this email: there are a lot of levels to this! If you want to become good at copywriting, whether it's to sell your own offers or for clients…

BECOME WELL READ.

I'm not kidding about this.

Not to brag (too much), but one of the major advantages I have as a copywriter is I've been studying on a wide range of topics and I've been a massive reader my entire life. This makes me very broad (not just deep) in what I know. It just gives me so much to be able to draw on to make connections and put into my copy for my clients that otherwise wouldn't be there.

Notice how I transition into the offer:

> There's no such thing as too many books, audios, or seminars! I STILL invest thousands each year in my education.

Kind of a self-serving paragraph, but it also happens to be true.

It's true that you have to be a constant lifelong learner (if you want to succeed). But I'm also opening that person up to investing in themselves, using the power of suggestion.

Note that as we get into the offer and call to action there's a time-limit. It's this week only. One of the most important things you can do is always juice up your offers with urgency. Give them a "why now." Otherwise, the slothful, distracted, and procrastinators of the world (which covers most people at some point or another) won't respond. You don't always have to do a deadline. And indeed, if you use my email methods and push the right emotional buttons like we're doing here, you might not need it. But it's still a good policy.

Alright, next:

> All of my most dedicated students use this.

This statement ticks a few boxes.

First, I am doing social proof with that. "My most dedicated students," what is that implying? One, I have a lot of students. "Most dedicated", the power of those two words is you want people to go, "Yeah, I'm dedicated too. I *should* be a dedicated student." And that's going to elevate them in that moment towards taking action. Plus we make the result sound easy like it's not a lot of work. It's a fairly simple thing. You just listen to these audios and you get the result.

As you can see, there are a lot of layers to that particular email.

Moving on...

EMAIL TYPE #5: The Q&A Email

This is a great type and one of my go-to's.

It's such an easy format, and one a lot of newspapers and magazines use with their "Dear Abby" type columns. It's therefore been proven to be a great way to get attention, and as a bonus, to get your emails read and to get sales! You're being posed a question and you're answering the question. There's absolutely nothing salesy about that. And so you're just going to give a little bit of content and then tease your offer.

Let's see how this works:

Subject: Are achy joints just a fact of aging?

Hi Conor,

Let's do a little Q&A action today.

Ok, here we go…

QUESTION: Dr. Kevin, I find as I'm getting older my joints are getting achier. Is this just a fact of aging, or is there something I can do about it?

KEVIN: Welcome to the club! Just kidding. Actually my answer might surprise you. A lot of the aches and pains we gripe about as we get older are due to (a) wear and tear, and (b) a slow buildup of inflammation.

This CAN be corrected with a mix of chiropractic adjustments using the BAK Method, lifestyle changes, and fixing muscle imbalances.

How far we take this depends on whether the cause is (1) your structure (i.e. you were made a certain way), or (2) the result of some kind of trauma (e.g. an injury, surgery, emotional stress, or chemical stress due to poor diet or medications).

The fun part?

If #2, in many cases it's possible to restore function 100% using the BAK Method!

It doesn't have to take long either.

When I met Sharon, she'd been in excruciating daily pain for 17 years. According to her doctors, she had arthritis. In performing my BAK Test on her I was able to quickly find the issue and the recipe to fix it. *We got rid of nearly 100% of her pain in the first appointment.*

Now let me ask you: did I cure arthritis in a single treatment?

I'm good but I'm not that good!

Arthritis was *not* her issue.

She was misdiagnosed.

Bottom line, you should never have to put up with achy joints or any other types of pain most people call "aging"!

If you haven't been to see me yet (or it's been a while)...and you want the solution to get out of pain and nix any nagging health problems...

Today May 31st is the *last day* to book a chiropractic adjustment with me and get *33% OFF a 30-minute massage* with our amazing massage therapist Olga Litvinova!

Join the patients who have already jumped on this lovely

offer. Reply to this email or call the office at (905) xxx-xxxx to book your appointment and discounted massage while spots last.

That's all for today.

Hope you enjoyed this.

If ever you have any questions reply and let me know. Your question may even get the "spotlight" in a future email!

Yours In Great Health,

Dr. Kevin

Let's recap.

The first obvious truth about doing these is the question should be something your market cares about. To a chiropractor's market, this is a question they care about. They have pain; that's one big reason they're interested in chiropractic. One thing this email does well is cover potential objections. This is another idea for writing emails. If there's a potential objection your market has, that could be an email in itself. You just bring up the objection and you talk about your response. This goes back to researching and understanding your market. You should have a list of all their potential objections; anything that might stop them (in their own mind) from taking you up on your offer. And you should cover those as much as possible in your sales letters and emails. Reduce that friction.

The more you remove reasons they may have for not buying what are they left with? If you've done your homework, *reasons FOR buying!*

Note this phrase:

> If #2, in many cases it's possible to restore function 100% using the BAK Method!

It doesn't have to take long either.

We've qualified it somewhat by saying "if this is you, you *can* get back to 100%".

They may be thinking, "yeah but this won't work for me." In fact, it's possible it will. Not only that, but it doesn't have to take long. There again, we're addressing what they're thinking. *Right, but I probably have to commit to a year of treatments through.* And with a lot of chiropractors that might be true. But this particular chiropractor bills himself as having the ability to get to the root of the problem quickly. To prove it, we share a little story about a long-suffering patient named Sharon.

You always want to be ten steps ahead. You want to know how they're going to react to any given statement.

Back to the email now, the takeaway for the reader is "bottom line you should never have to put up with achy joints or any other types of pain most people call aging". This is great because we're giving people an opportunity for thinking differently about something. A lot of people really do think that, "Oh I'm just getting older and that's why my joints hurt and I should just kind of accept it." Whereas we're saying, "Hey, that's not true." And actually it isn't true. There's a lot that can be done for joint pain. Their mind begins to open up to new possibilities. So we've hopefully made them more receptive to our offer as well.

Good statement:

> Join the patients who have already jumped on this lovely offer.

This is how to do social proof without referencing a testimonial or anything.

We're saying other people are going for this. And again having explained social proof in other parts of this book, it's really just making your offer "safe" because other people are going for it and this helps justify its value.

This is important too.

In your call to action you MUST…

Tell Them <u>Exactly</u> What To Do.

Do not miss this part.

Make it crystal clear in your call to action exactly what steps to take. *Reply to this email* or *call this number* or *go to this link*. Whatever it is, you need to spell it out. Tell people in no uncertain terms what to do next. Don't leave them guessing. If there's even the slightest confusion about this, it will cost you sales. You must lead them all the way there.

Finally, at the end I've solicited more questions. It's a great way to do it. *If you ever have any questions reply and let me know*. Questions are great fodder for emails and other content. And a good excuse to send another email that's going to make you more sales, by the way.

One more point: people do like that spotlight. It makes them feel important if their question gets featured. You have almost a sort of celebrity with your list and for them seeing their name or their question featured in some of your content is a cool thing.

Alright, expanding on the theme a little bit, below is a "bonus" example of how to cover objections in your emails:

Subject: How does the BAK Test Work? (A skeptic challenges me)

Hi Conor,

A subscriber writes…

"I get that your BAK Test is useful, but how can it be right every time? I mean, come on!"

We have a skeptic in our midst!

Personally, I love the patients who are skeptical at first.

(They're usually the ones who have the best outcomes!)

I know it sounds crazy, but the BAK Test *is* right every single time when it comes to diagnosing the *true* cause of your symptoms.

Working with top professional athletes, I can't afford to be wrong. They want me to get them "game ready"...*now*...or they'll find someone else who can do it. The reason I'm in demand is because I can get to the root of things *quickly*.

Here's how the "magic" works (it's not magic):

The BAK Test is a test that can be done on ANY pair of muscles.

We compare movement on both sides. Then, knowing the physiology of how muscles and nerves interact, we can pinpoint patterns that explain your symptoms. Also, because it's simple and repeatable, we can instantly confirm its results. The test therefore reveals the custom recipe for how to deliver care that gives you the kind of fast results you want.

For example:

Marcus was an elite level track athlete trying to qualify for the *Canadian Olympic Team.*

His problem was he was no longer progressing in his training. His coach said, "I can see it...something's limiting him." The BAK Test showed me what that was. *In 10 minutes* he was back on the track and his coach could already see the improvement.

I could go on.

I have THOUSANDS more examples that prove the BAK Test's effectiveness.

It's even been medically certified.

And it doesn't just work for athletes, it works for anyone.

If you haven't experienced it yet, I have but one question:

What are you waiting for?

Tomorrow is the *last day to take advantage of a free, no-obligation consultation with me* (and pick up your free copy of my book at your visit). After that, it goes back up to full price.

Book your appointment before time runs out.

Simply call (905) xxx-xxxx or go here to book your appointment:

[link]

Don't put this off.

Life's too short to not be at your best…even for a second.

Make it a great afternoon!

Dr. Kevin

P.S. Laying down a few more bread crumbs for the skeptics to follow…

"I have to admit that I was a sceptic about the chiropractic treatment. Furthermore – I was a mess. Through proper

alignment, Dr Kevin restored my balance and my life. Thank you for putting the spring back in my step Dr Kevin." – C.M.

Another subject line that got a very high open rate:

How does the BAK Test work? (A skeptic challenges me)

I continue bringing this up because becoming good at writing subject lines is one of the most important skills for success with email marketing. Without your emails getting opened, they aren't getting read. Without them getting read, you won't be getting as many sales!

What this subject line does is number one, it's a *question,* which is inherently non-salesy. But note the bit in between parentheses at the end of the subject line "a skeptic challenges me". It intrigues for the same reason people watch reality TV – there's a voyeuristic aspect to it. And it implies some kind of drama or confrontation, which is interesting. This = getting your emails opened and read.

'Nuff said.

Now watch this:

> We have a skeptic in our midst!
>
> Personally, I love the patients who are skeptical at first.
>
> (They're usually the ones who have the best outcomes!)

What I've done with these three statements is very powerful. Look, there are going to be a certain percentage of people on your list who are skeptical. Here, we're both encouraging and inviting their skepticism with these three short sentences. Almost to the point where we're saying if you're skeptical, good, even better because you are the category of person that is most likely to get the best outcome from this. If you can imply that the more skeptical a person is, the better, then anyone who is skeptical can begin to let their guard down. You're telling them "if you're skeptical, you stand to benefit". Not only have you acknowledged their skepticism, and made it ok, but you've made it almost a condition of doing business with you!

Next:

> Working with top professional athletes, I can't afford to be wrong. They want me to get them "game ready"...*now*...or they'll find someone else who can do it. The reason I'm in demand is because I can get to the root of things *quickly*.

This is what I call a "proof" paragraph.

First, there's the fact that he works with top professional athletes. Then, there's the common sense truth that if he can't deliver, he's out. This, together with the story of the Olympic track athlete infuses the copy with an air of believability. You may also notice we're clear about how this method *doesn't just work for athletes*. Okay? Very important. We've mentioned professional athletes and Olympic athletes to create credibility, but we really are targeting the average person with this particular email. You don't want people to think, "Oh, well, I'm not an athlete. So that eliminates me."

Final point:

Wherever possible I like to use a testimonial that speaks to whatever specific benefit I'm covering in a given email. If I'm writing an email that's about pregnant women, I like to put a testimonial in the email that was from a pregnant woman. I want a testimonial that sort of proves my point. In the example above the first line in the testimonial is, "I have to admit I was a skeptic". You can see how it speaks to the central theme of this particular email.

All right, trucking along here...

EMAIL TYPE #6: The Cautionary Tale

This bad boy is one of my favorite types of emails.

Again, stories are huge because they're naturally entertaining. Do I sound like a broken record yet? In the cautionary tale, we're telling the story to warn them about something. And this is usually something that happened to someone in your market or a horror story where you can list all these horrible things that people in your market are dealing with. Keeping your emails focused on their problems as opposed to your product or service is the way that you're never going to lose their attention. You're never going to bore someone as long as you're staying in their "world" and talking about their problems.

With that in mind, let's serve up the next course:

Subject: The Legend of The Drunken Chiropractor

Dear Conor,

There's a style of martial arts known as Drunken Boxing. It was made famous by Jackie Chan in the movie *Legend of Drunken Master*. Fighters in this style sway and weave, imitating the movements of a drunkard.

Thanks to my recent bout of vertigo, I've discovered why 'drunken chiropractic' probably won't make it onto Hollywood's radar anytime soon.

In a Kung Fu match, you can keep your opponents off balance with this unorthodox, stumbling style. When treating a patient, on the other hand, it doesn't help to feel like you're buzzed, and on a boat in the middle of the ocean.

The vertigo was a result of a virus that already had my number. And guess what? Instead of listening to my body and taking some time off, Captain Seamus here decided to push through and keep working.

I guess as a health professional that makes me guilty of not drinking my own Kool-Aid in this case.

I share this confession as an opportunity for you to think about where you might be burning the candle at both ends, too. Here's a good test: when's the last time you went for a walk just to *enjoy* going for a walk, and not to get somewhere, or for exercise?

Good one to ponder.

In our busy world it can be easy to fall into the trap doing, doing, doing and never taking time to just BE. If we're not careful we devolve into human 'doings', and forget that we're human 'beings' who need a certain amount of stillness and quiet to thrive.

Anyway, take it for what it's worth.

I figure we can all use a reminder like this from time to time.

Speaking of reminders (how's that for a segue?), there are just two weeks left of 2018. Have you gotten the most out of your benefits plan at work? Did you know that our services here at the clinic are covered by most health plans?

Your sweat equity at the office is paying for your benefits

either way.

Why not use them? Book a massage, or see one of the physios for a nagging pain – your company's buying. But hurry, time is running out and it's our busiest time of the year. Hit reply or call the clinic at (416) xxx-xxxx to book your appointment before there are no more spots left.

And I hope my cautionary tale reaches you.

Health is all about balance – literally, sometimes.

Yours In Great Health,

In the subject "the legend of..." implies a story and "drunken chiropractor" is just a weird idea.

There's a lot of contrast in that idea and it's just kind of bizarre. Finally, it's a take-off of a movie title. Spinning movie titles and book titles creatively is a great way to come up with subject lines. These are the kinds of things that get attention and get your emails opened; lots of contrast, lots of weird, atypical subject lines. That's how you're going to do it.

The offer is more of a reminder (since it was the end of the year when we sent this out) that chiropractic is covered under most benefits plans. Because a lot of people are trying to use up their benefits at that point, it also happens to be the busiest time of year for many chiropractors. It's just an easy way to create scarcity and urgency all at the same time, which is a great way to make sales. Once you have both of those, simply tell them very specifically what to do. *Hit reply, call the clinic*.

Alright now for the Grand Finale of our email types:

EMAIL TYPE #7: The Inspirational Email

I think one reason I like doing these so much is heck, I'm just an inspirational guy!

What can I say?

Joking aside, these ones do come very naturally to me. And I believe (others may disagree with me) people are starved for this kind of thing. They want to be entertained, yes. And they want to be inspired. They want to feel good. There's so much bad news out there. When you can be that beacon of light, people really appreciate that and gravitate towards it. It's worthwhile to get good at doing this kind of thing.

Let's look at an example:

Subject: The Governator's secret to winning at email

I've been ruminating on the Arnold Schwarzenegger clip I shared earlier this week.

(I link to it below.)

All the books, audios, and courses I've ingested have more or less turned my brain into a search bar for self-help content. Re: Arnie's comment on it being ok to fail, the software of my memory turned up this little ditty...

I recall someone saying that the most remarkable thing about Fred Smith, the founder of FedEx, was his ability to laugh about failure.

Whenever one of their initiatives flopped, and many did, he'd get a wry smile on his face, shake his head and go "wow that *really* didn't work."

Then he'd simply say "what next?"

During my brief stint in stand-up comedy, I wrote pages full of setups and punchlines. I quickly realized about 10% of it was funny. The catch is the only way to know *which* 10% is to stand in front of people and let 90% of your stuff bomb. Do that ten times and you wind up with five minutes of material that will do reasonably well with most audiences.

Call it *accelerated* failing.

That's the great thing about email. As a format, it's very forgiving. Most emails aren't runaway successes. Some might not resonate. But there's always the next one. And if you have even a tiny bit of good will built up with your reader, they'll quickly forget about any duds.

The only way you lose is if you stop.

Going back to the comedy thing for a moment, there were many times a joke landed and all I got back were crickets. It never occurred to me those could be reasons to stop. I just figured that was the process.

In fact, I'll go you one further...

I embrace failing.

Because the more I fail, the smarter I get.

Besides, if that's your approach, and every attempt results in either a win or a lesson...

Do we ever truly fail?

Here's that video:

https://www.youtube.com/watch?v=qNpEFf0I60M

Happy Failing,

Conor Kelly

P.S. Go here:

=>Double Your Customer Base With The FREE 4-Week Challenge.

This is a curiosity-provoking subject line because of the famous person being referenced.

If you can reference celebrities in your subject lines, those get attention too. Basically what I'm doing here is talking about some wisdom from Fred Smith, the founder of FedEx. And how someone who knew him said it's his ability to laugh at failure was really what made him stand out. Then I go on to talk about standup comedy and how it's the same kind of thing.

It's being able to fail quickly.

Or "fail forward" as I've heard it called.

And email lends itself to this. That's what you want to do with this email type; tie it back to what you do. The great thing about an inspirational email is you're creating a state. When people feel inspired, it's a platform for them to take action. I've got my call to action down at the bottom and as you can see, it can be as simple as *P.S. Go here*. I was bouncing to a sales page in this particular case, and there's a straight benefit to get them to click.

Notice something.

This is an email in which I haven't mentioned anything about my product or my service in the email. I've just sort of given them a thought provoking, inspiring email. And then at the bottom I have my call to action. That's the only point I bring things back to what I'm selling. I don't suggest you do this all the time, but when you do, not only is it under the radar from a selling and persuading perspective, but it's a welcome relief from the focus on tips or problems.

The key to all this is…

Never Be <u>Boring</u>.

Use contrast as much as possible.

Mix it up. You want to keep them guessing a little bit as to what's coming next. Lots of variety and contrast both within your emails and from one email to the next will do the trick. Do short one day, long the next. Inspirational one day, then a horror story the next. And so on.

I think you get the picture.

Chapter 6

Biggest Email Myths & Mistakes

"Would you jump into a pool without water? No.
The splash is what keeps you alive. Splash is life."
– Gina Linetti, *Brooklyn 99*

Here's the story:

In the early days of my business, I was doing some cold calls to drum up clients. One real estate agent in my area had mailed out a booklet with coupons to some of the neighborhood businesses, which I thought was a great idea. So I called him up. I said, "You seem like a guy who's open to some new ideas about marketing…"

I asked him if he used email, and he did. But he was more or less doing what every real estate agent does which is to send yawningly dry market updates or only email when they have a new listing. I suggested we try something different to help him stand out. Even add some (gasp!) *entertainment* to spice things up.

His reply?

> "I don't know…that can be kitschy."

Based on the reaction of my mastermind group when I told this story (it sent them rushing to the Googletionary to look up "kitschy") I should probably help you out:

> **kitschy** *adj* considered to be in poor taste because of excessive garishness or sentimentality.

"Cheesy" might be a good synonym.

Now by no means am I proposing you become the email equivalent of a monkey that plays the accordion. And you do not need to bowl folks over with your charisma as your humble author is wont to do (you try keeping a lid on all this animal magnetism). However, adding "splashes" of personality is one of the key ways we attract interest.

A Lot Of Business Owners Are Scared To Death Of Looking "Unprofessional".

That's not what we're talking about here.

Just be a person. That's the essence of personality. Don't be plain icing. Add sprinkles of "you" on top. *Retail Marketing Institute* recently wrote that 70.9% of customers would STOP doing business with someone and go somewhere else if it was more FUN. You see, people will *say* they want to be informed but the truth is they'd rather be entertained. There's no amount of information that will make a video go viral. That's why your best case scenario is to "infotain" your list with a smattering of both info and fun.

This also lets you…

Email More Often And "Get Away With" Selling In Every Email, too!

I'm serious about this, too.

And what of our real estate agent who so wantonly spurned my muscular ways? I guarantee he's costing himself sales (and probably a lot of notoriety too). In the words of advertising legend and original "mad man" David Ogilvy (who the character of Don Draper in Mad Men was based on):

> *Tell the truth but make truth fascinating. You know, you can't bore people into buying your product. You can only interest them in buying it.*

Splash is life.

The rest of this chapter will deal with a few more common email marketing myths, mistakes, and the just-plain-misguided or downright-batty thinking most business owners become infected with when it comes to this sweet science.

Like for starters...

"But my clients don't want to hear from me by email."

Correct.

They don't want boring, corporate, blatantly self-promotional emails carpet-bombing their already cluttered inbox. If your current emails are simply telling your customers and prospects about promotions and things going on in your business, you shouldn't be sending 1-2x per month, you should *never* be sending. Why? Because the best email marketing programs make the emails about the customer, not the business. They speak to their interests, attracting their attention and then gently compel them to buy more of your products and services. It's a win-win. The customers love reading the emails, and your business wins because every email you send increases profits and revenue.

And back to the point I made earlier about Dan Kennedy and what he calls "marketing incest". When you do these things and you're the only one in your market doing them, you stand out! If mistake #1 is being dry, boring, and overly professional (or focused on your own products and services vs. your customers' problems), then related to that is putting too much hard content or information in your newsletters and not doing an "infotaining" mix.

Next, beware…

The "Social Media Guru" Line-Dance That'll Have You Spinning In Circles!

Maybe you've seen this.

They're sometimes called "goodwill" emails. People like Gary Vaynerchuk ("Jab, jab, jab, punch" is his famous line) expound this feel-good theory; that you want to send a bunch of content and relationship based "nurture" emails before you ask for the sale. And I think those people are full of crap to be honest with you. Apart from that, last I checked Gary V is not an email guy. If you care about your audience, you must at least acknowledge that sending them an email is not going to change their life. Getting involved with your service or your program or your product is the solution they need.

When you frame it thus, you have a responsibility (again, if you care about them), to share with them what you have, and put it in front of them as much as possible. Emails that are straight content, people tend not to read anyway. They go "That looks interesting," then put them aside for later but never come back to them. Ones that are so-called "pitching", because they're talking about concerns they have right now they tend to think "Well okay, let me just have a peek at this".

How Often Should You Email Your List?

I may be controversial in this.

Many experts say *daily* is a must.

The real answer is it depends on your market.

There are certain sensibilities about what's going on in your market that you need to be aware of, but for the most part I find that the correct answer to that question is a number far higher than what you're comfortable with! Like I said, many of the top email educators insist it has to be daily. And for many businesses that may be overkill. But rarely would I suggest less than 1x/week. 2-3x/week is better. Most of the businesses that I go into and tell them "we're going to do two, three emails a week", they freak out and they're like, "oh my God, that's insane…isn't that excessive?" The biggest refrain I hear from people is they don't want to annoy their customers.

But this misses the point.

If you're sending crap or just a pretty newsletter with an offer or the latest news about your company, but it's not about your customers and things that they care about…or it's not done in a fun or interesting way… then obviously yes, they're not going to want them. But if you're sending them things that they like, that are completely different, they get into it and get engaged with what you're doing to the point where they actually start to look forward to reading your emails.

You may even find if you miss a day or a few days people go "Hey, what happened to you? I'm missing my daily fix of your content." The whole *I'll annoy them* fear and frame of reference needs to be shifted. You're projecting how you'd feel in that situation. Whereas if you put the customer first and you send them stuff that's relevant to them that you think they'll like and that is about their problems and concerns and all that kind of stuff – different ballgame.

And when you do, frequency can be potentially unlimited.

I'm not even exaggerating.

Why Email Swipes Are Useless

I learned a lesson about swiping copy early on.

Not because I've ever actually used copy I swiped from someone else. But I'd hired a coaching company that helps fitness businesses with their marketing. They had hundreds of success stories and members raving about the results from their "done-for-you" campaigns. And they were great coaches, don't get me wrong. I learned a ton. But the campaigns they provided were templates. Even though I was hearing about trainers in other markets doing ridiculous numbers with these email and letter sequences, I'd plug them into my marketing, send them out and get crickets back.

True story.

I figured out pretty quickly that whatever they were doing just wasn't resonating with my market. I needed to put in the leg work to figure out my market and speak to their unique sensibilities. That's where a lot of entrepreneurs who attempt this trip up. They look at what other email marketers are doing and either blatantly rip them off or try to imitate their style. They're using somebody else's voice but they're never really finding their own unique voice that's going to help them to stand out.

It doesn't work.

Next:

The Zig Ziglar Email Secret That Leads To Fat Margins!

One day I went for a walk.

As I was walking, a squirrel accosted me. What I mean is it skittered over – while I was in full stride – planted itself in front of me, sat up on its hind legs, and stared me down. I've never seen a squirrel behave so brazenly.

So I stopped.

I said hi.

(It seemed like the thing to do.)

My furry friend then cautiously crept forward, even touching my shoe. I knew he was looking for food. I said "sorry bud, don't have any," and went on about my merry way. What struck me about this close encounter of the rodent kind is that he was the fattest squirrel I'd ever seen. And why not? He's clearly not afraid to ask for his meal. It reminded me of Zig Ziglar's famous quote:

"Timid salespeople have skinny children."

The point is to ASK for what you want.

The email marketing equivalent is having a clear and highly visible call-to-action for your reader to follow. When someone reads your emails, do they know what you want them to DO? If there's even the slightest bit of confusion about this, you won't get many sales/leads/appointments. Squirrel-food for thought...

Thus, let the rule be...

Have A Call To Action In Every Email!

There's a call to action...in action.

You don't have to ask for a sale. You could ask them to reply, book a call, or opt in for some type of content or new funnel they're not on yet. You can ask for referrals or leads. You can ask them to write a review or support a charity you're involved with in exchange for an "ethical bribe". The point is to ask, ask, ask. As Best-Selling Author and co-creator of the *Chicken Soup For The Soul* series of books Jack Canfield says, "become an askhole". My early email mentors had a slightly different take on this; "no email goes out without an offer in it."

Alright, next thing...

Perfect Is The Enemy Of Done.

I remember one client in particular.

The first email I sent over, not only did he make edits, but it got bounced back and forth on email threads with other members of his team. At one point, when it seemed we had a draft he was happy with, he brought in some other outside advisor to comment! Not even someone on his team. This all happened in an interval when I was off email, by the way.

When I logged on and saw this madness, all I wrote was this:

"NO MORE EDITS! GET IT OUT."

Perfectionism is truly a disease.

Especially when it comes to email. This may come as a big shock to you, but your emails, whether they are perfect or not, will be a lot more effective sitting in your prospect's inbox than in your "drafts" folder! I can't guarantee you'll get tons of sales and happy responses if you send it out, but I can absolutely guarantee you'll get none of that if you don't.

Why Spellcheck Might Be Killing Your Sales

Here's a strange story for you.

A few years ago a company called Porter Stansberry Research used a plain Jane video sales letter to sell a whopping $200M worth of subscriptions to their Investment Advisory. The video was called *End of America*. (You can watch it on YouTube if you're curious.)

I mean this thing is ghetto. It's black and white, and conspicuous by its lack of images…in fact, there are no graphics at all, just words. The late, great Eugene Schwartz, the Granddaddy of the modern copywriter was famous for saying:

"The ugly thing in the world of beauty stands out."

Good one to keep in mind.

Similarly, when most businesses are sending slick-looking, branded HTML newsletters with fancy graphics, your plain text emails complete with typos and all stand out. I'd go as far as to say that trying to make your emails 'professional' is the kiss of death. For one, professional is common, drab and uninteresting. And it screams corporate – a good way to ensure no one cares about your emails. Finally, many of the newsletters I review are busy, click-baited hot-messes that lack a clear call to action.

The Best Emails Are Simple And Personal.

Like a message from a friend.

And most people that are not corporate mouthpieces write in a conversational tone, use imperfect grammar, and can't spell worth a dime. As hard as it will be for the graphic designers of the world to swallow, looking good and making sales – sometimes – are competing ideals.

Next, a caution…

Do <u>Not</u> Put These Two Words In Your Offers.

While back I sent my client their email promo.

I'd crafted a fine offer. Put some "muscle" on it (i.e. spiced it up with a few psychological triggers to help folks buy). Then, I entrusted them with its care. When it landed in my inbox, they'd added a bunch of words without telling me. Where I'd made a point of emphasizing this was an exclusive offer to our subscribers…tacked on was the statement *please share this with anyone you think would benefit.*

In our next meeting I queried, "so…who added this bit?" The business owner cautiously admitted "that might have been me". I said, "yeah…don't do that."

The two words not to put in your offers?

>   *Please share.*

Here's why:

One, exclusivity is one of said 'psychological triggers that help folks buy'. Humans are enticed by *access*. And our nervous systems are wired to think of what is rare as valuable. If just about anyone can have your offers, there's a good chance no one will want them.

Two, it can come off as needy and hurt your positioning with your prospect. In fact, using *please DON'T share* often packs more punch.

Finally, to paraphrase Perry Marshall, every time you hit 'send' you are training people to read your next email. You do this mainly by keeping your content interesting, relevant, or entertaining in some way. But bigging up the exclusivity of your offers doesn't hurt either.

Who wants to miss out on a great deal?

The only time asking readers to forward your emails can work is if you frame it as "I'm on a mission to help" as I did once with a client who did magnesium infusions to cure headaches and migraines. The treatment is (a) ridiculously effective (one woman got rid of a 17-year headache her first go), and (b) everyone knows at least one person with this problem. Such was my logic. Most offers aren't like that.

Anyway, take it for what it's worth – the psychology of this works everywhere, not just in email.

People like exclusivity.

Why not give it to them?

Chapter 7

Creating Offers That Compel Response

"You should think more about how to 'sweeten' your offer than any other aspect of writing copy." – Gary Halbert

Here's something almost any small business can do.

Make a deal with a massage place or a spa. They will agree to "sponsor" a half-price offer which you'll use as a bonus to incentivize your email subscribers to take action on something.

I've rarely not seen this work.

Imagine your car mechanic had an offer, "half-price massage with the clinic next door while you wait for your car – this month only." Would you find that compelling? Most folks would. Or it could be a personal trainer, "book a 5 session pack and get a free massage – this week only". Or a computer repair services place. Or a chiropractor. I honestly think EVERY small business should test this.

Here's the point:

A half-price massage (or free) is almost always a strong offer.

As is a spa treatment.

Or anything else that feels like "spoiling" and which many people would ordinarily resist treating themselves with.

What's in it for the massage place? Customers. Granted, you need to find a partner who "gets it." But they're out there. Remember, every business needs more customers. Let's say you have a customer list of 1,000 and ten of them take you up on your offer…that is ten very high-quality leads for the massage place at no up-front cost and at a total cost far less than they would otherwise have to invest to acquire the same number of new leads. PLUS, they're leveraging the trust you've built with your list.

They couldn't buy this kind of promotion.

Bottom line, getting your readers to take action is about one thing:

The Right Incentives!

Always incentivize your readers to take action.

Why, with everything they've got going on, should they stop what they're doing, resist the urge to click away or put it off, and take some proposed action now? The answer to this is in your offers. And it's the second most important ingredient in your success (having a qualified list of subscribers – Gary Halbert's "starving crowd" – is the first).

Four Simple Ways To Do Offers In Email

Here they are:

1. The Free Offer (e.g. a consultation, or call)
2. The Discount
3. Bonuses
4. Guarantees (and non-guarantees)

First, the free offer:

The free offer could be an offer of content, as in *download this free report* or *get my new email micro-course on x*. These are used mainly when you want to segment your list and get a portion of your customers or subscribers to whet their appetite a little for a new product or service offering that's coming down the line.

For our purposes, let's focus on what a lot of services do, which is a consultation or a call of some kind. This particular offer is the most common go-to for someone who has a service and needs to do a little discovery and qualify people first before bringing them onboard. Basically, it's an opportunity to get on the phone with your potential buyer or client, diagnose their needs, and if there's a fit, put them into one of your plans or programs. In this case you'd make the sale over the phone, or in-person depending on the type of business you're in.

There are a number of ways you can do this.

One way that I happen to like is to tie your offer of a consultation to whatever the lesson was in that particular email. You give them only a brief overview of the tip or trick in the body of the email. Then, you tease the reveal of the rest of that secret.

Let's say you give an example of a trick or a technique you've used in the past to help a client. This is probably one of the easiest ways to do this. You hint at what the trick is without fully going into how they would do it on their own. Next, let them know this is something you share only with clients, and if you book your free consultation by the deadline, then I will reveal the rest of this trick.

In one email I talked about a "magic" nine-word email I used to net a client 10K in contracts.

Here's how I worded that offer:

> There's a secret 9-word email being used by the world's most elite marketers that is cashing in BIG for a few lucky list owners. The best story I heard so far is one of my colleagues used it to sell a $50M super yacht.

Yes I know how weird that sounds.

But it's also true.

There was a bit more back and forth required to close the deal, but that simple 9-word message initiated it.

Here's the catch:

I've seen this work like gangbusters in some markets, and utterly flop in others.

What those "magic" 9 words are...

Whether your industry is a fit...

And literally dozens more high-level email tactics and strategies...

All are to be found "inside" your *Free Brainstorm Call* with Yours Muscularly:

http://calendly.com/conorkel/emailincome

It's simple enough to do, and it works.

Another thing you can do is tie your free offer to a bonus of some kind, e.g. *if you book your consultation before such and such a date, or before space runs out*, then you'll get some free thing, or some half price thing. Or it could be a paid consultation plus bonus. That's another way to do it. Here's an example from the chiropractic niche:

This month:

If you're not currently under care, and you'd like some help reducing pain or any health symptoms, book an assessment (or re-assessment) at the regular price and get a **free 2-month supply of USANA Vitamin C & D** as my gift to you!

Think of this as your "double-whammy" against all the colds and flus that are so prevalent this time of year.

Simply reply to this email or call the office at (416) xxx-xxxx to book your appointment while spots last.

Offer Expires November 30th.

Again, offers like this are very straightforward and easy to dream up.

Second type of offer is a **discount**.

Now this is an obvious play. You can take anywhere from 10% to 30%, to 90% off a product that you're selling. And that way you can tie it to a deadline, as in *this week only*, making it a very limited time offer. It's a great, simple way to do it. Who doesn't like saving money? People love to feel like they're getting a deal.

One thing you can actually do with this, and I mentioned it a little earlier in the chapter on Sales Letters, is to sell what we call the "reason for the deal". If you have a strong reason for why you're giving such a big discount, you also have plausible scarcity. In the baseball niche I once sold a product that teaches drills with a particular training tool, and the offer was they'd get the training tool for free with the videos. However, as we explained, we had a limited number because we were only able to negotiate 1,000 from the manufacturer at this special price.

That allows you to tack on a lot of scarcity and urgency as well.

Here's one example of how I'd do this for a free + shipping deal:

We'll send you your mini band and the workout poster that shows your pitcher exactly what to do absolutely FREE. No strings attached. Nothing up my sleeve. You just pitch in the cost of shipping.

Call it a perk of being one of my VIP subscribers. ☺

There *is* one small catch.

We could only get X amount.

We went to bat *hard* for you to bring you the best possible deal because we believe the mini band is a "must-have" tool for any pitcher.

And let's just say XYZ Company is VERY stingy with giving discounts.

So we can't keep giving them away free forever.

Pitchers absolutely love these mini bands.

Any serious pitcher, or concerned dad/coach is going to want one.

Click the button below to order yours RIGHT NOW while supplies last.

You can come up with these all day.

When it comes to services, this is just a personal preference, but especially if you're an individual freelancer or a professional, a chiropractor, a dentist, a coach or consultant, that kind of thing, I wouldn't discount much – or often. For positioning purposes, I don't think it's a great idea for you to discount your service because that is your time. You could certainly discount, for example, the initial consultation, but in general terms I don't think you want to discount your actual service. For that reason, I would tend to prefer doing bonuses for services.

Rather than lowering my price, it's *if you commit today. then I'll add in this*. For example, I'll do your sales letter, but if you move forward today, I am also going to include a six email affiliate launch series. Again, the idea is to sweeten the deal.

This brings us to the third way to do offers: **bonuses**.

As we mentioned above, with the half-price massage example, this can be a bonus that you have, that you drum up from somewhere, or something that you get from a joint venture partner. That involves getting someone who is willing to give you a bonus that you can share with your customers in exchange for getting them in front of your list, paying them a commission, or giving them the opportunity to get new customers. It all depends on how you want to negotiate that one.

The concept of a bonus is...

If You Buy X, I'll Also Give You Y.

It's another excuse to tie urgency to what you're doing.

In case you haven't noticed, that's a pretty important piece. You want to have some kind of urgency and scarcity because, once we get into action drivers, you'll see that it's one of the main ways to get people to take action on what you're offering.

Another trick is to sell the bonus. You almost want to treat the bonus as its own separate product, and give it as much airtime in your "pitch" as your main offer, and sometimes even more. Sometimes your main offer might be something your list of subscribers is already very familiar with, like if it's a free consultation or whatever. Don't balk at spending time really going deep on what they get from the bonus, and making it sound really enticing.

Finally, bonuses are something that, if you have something on hand, some content you're not using, unused videos, eBooks that you haven't published...*presto*, there's your bonus. Also, not necessary but if it can be something that has a proven retail value, that's always great because you can then say, "This is sold elsewhere for such and such a price." That really ramps up the perceived value of your offer.

Bonuses are also fairly easy to create.

You can create one even by talking an audio on a certain subject that you know your subscribers are interested in. With one client, I interviewed him for twenty minutes on a specific subject that I thought was a hot topic to his followers, and we recorded it. The result was a new product that we gave a title to, and that we could offer as a limited time bonus.

Take a look:

> P.S. Your personal bias for action today could be as simple as to grab your copy of my bestselling book *I Have The Watch* by going here.
>
> If you buy it before October 30th and send me your receipt, I'll send you a special 20-minute video interview I recorded called "Engage Your People, Or Die" that contains some of my best "shotgun" tricks for quickly getting your team on board when your survival depends on it...because it does!
>
> This exclusive recording is NOT for sale anywhere.
>
> But it's yours FREE if you buy the book today and send me your receipt by October 30th at 11:59 PM.

Number four is to have a **unique guarantee**.

We've covered guarantees already, but just to make the point, if you do have a good one, or a unique one, it's good to lead with. That means it doesn't have to be only in your sales letter, it can be spelled out in your emails. You can even have one email that's just all about the specifics of the guarantee.

The other thing you can do is have a **non-guarantee**. What do I mean by that? It's where you go into your offer and instead of hyping it up and saying, "I'll give you twice your money back," or "Return it any time for the rest of your life, no questions asked," you can instead say very pointedly, "I don't guarantee this."

Use an example of a client that got a result and say, "Not everybody is going to get this result. I don't guarantee this, but if you can live with that, and you understand that results may vary, here is my offer." That's been successful for me as well. I think the big reason for that is just because that candidness, that takeaway is a great way to build trust. Ninety percent of motivating anyone is based on trust. So I think that kind of honesty really plays well.

See here:

> My decidedly un-hyped offer:
>
> If you'd like me to perform one of my signature *Instant Copy Upgrade* reviews on your sales letter, website, or email campaign, reply to this email with a few details and a link to, or an attachment with item in question.
>
> Once I've had a peak...
>
> And if it's a fit, I'll reply with next steps.
>
> You'll be getting very specific, very detailed secrets I've used to help clients like Matt as much as double their

web conversions...all for a relatively small one-time investment (which, if you reply today only, I'll credit toward your fee should you decide to hire me to do a rewrite.)

Two things:

1. I make no guarantees about this.

I know my stuff. You'll see. But much of this has to do with the dynamics of your market and your offer, none of which is within my control.

2. If you don't currently have a list...or *buyers*...or leads coming in...you'll learn a lot, but it probably won't help you much in the short term. The best candidate for this is someone who's already doing marketing, getting traffic of some kind, and has at least some sales.

Alright, let's wrap up this already very productive chapter.

You can also pick and choose, and do any combination of the four, and you should. You really want to spend time on your offers. The reality is most people probably don't spend the time that they should on this. Like the Godfather,

Make Them An Offer They Can't Refuse.

Well, don't go putting any guns to anyone's head!

You know what I mean.

How can you sweeten it to the point where it just seems ridiculous or stupid to not take advantage of this offer? It's just a no-brainer. You wouldn't really combine a free offer with a discount, but you can combine a discount with a bonus and a guarantee, and mash them all together to make one super offer, or a free offer with a bonus and a guarantee. Just take all of these, throw them into a mish mash and brainstorm lots of different variations and see what comes out.

That's the basis of success, more so than your copy even.

There's an old rule called the **40-40-20 Rule**. Your success is going to be based 40% on your list, 40% on your offer, and 20% on the actual copy. That shows you how huge the offer is right there. Now my personal preference would be to say, I'd probably skew it a little more towards the list and your relationship with your list, but absolutely the offer is 30, if not 40% of the success of your promotion, maybe more in some cases if you have a really good offer.

In the next chapter, I'm going to show you how to take your offers, and put them on steroids!

Chapter 8

Key Drivers Of Action

"In classical times when Cicero had finished speaking, the people said, 'How well he spoke' but when Demosthenes had finished speaking, they said, 'Let us march.'" -- Adlai Stevenson, *introducing John F. Kennedy in 1960*

Next we're going to talk about **action drivers** in email.

There are a lot of different action drivers – also known as "psychological triggers" – that you could be using in your emails to make them more persuasive and to compel people to take action. But my promise with this book is to keep things simple. So with that in mind, there are really only four psychological triggers or action drivers that you need to care about.

First, a story:

One of my early teachers in business is T. Harv Eker. He's best known as the founder of Peak Potentials, a business and personal development training company. He's also the author of the book *Secrets of the Millionaire Mind*, which I highly recommend, by the way.

Harv had opened one of the first fitness equipment stores in Toronto.

In his seminars he tells the story of what he did when he first opened the store. First, he leased himself a small space. They were selling a particular variation of a rowing machine. And what he did was position the sales counter and the rower demonstration near the front of this already small space. The result was that at any given time, you couldn't have more than a few people inside, whether it was for a demo, or for signing paperwork and completing a purchase.

Not long before their grand opening they'd secured a one-page cover story in one of Toronto's major newspapers. When they opened there was a pretty major queue. Now don't forget, only two or three or however many people could fit inside the store to begin with! Before too long not only was there a giant lineup but a crowd started to form.

This reached such a fever pitch that the police insisted the store hire pay duties (off duty police officers) to do crowd control. The "side-effect" of all this was that people came along and they would see this massive crowd gathering and they'd say, "What the heck is going on here?" Of course, they'd be immediately drawn in to try to figure it out and even get interested themselves. But more importantly, the crowd created so much more desire that…

It Almost Turned Into A *Feeding Frenzy* For His Products!

Good side-effect.

That's a really good example of what we call *social proof*.

And it's one of the action drivers to think about. Dan Kennedy famously cautions clients against what he termed "empty parking lot syndrome". Let's say, for example, he had a chiropractor client. He'd go as far as to have that client ensure that the parking lot was always filled with nice cars, even if it meant getting friends to park their cars there or paying people to park their cars there. The bottom line is people don't want to do business with someone who has no clients.

Everybody wants to do business with someone who's in demand. Social proof essentially "vets" that person or that business. A lot of times it really shouldn't, but it still does. That's because it's a cognitive bias; a shortcut your brain uses to save on energy-expensive thinking. Social proof helps verify that the person or the business is, for lack of a better word, safe. If lots of other people choose to do business with this person, it's likely that they're a good choice to make.

Again, not always true, but you see what I'm getting at.

That, in a nutshell, is how the whole social proof thing works.

Top 4 Action-Drivers To Focus On In Emails

We'll talk about each of them a little bit more in a second.

But they are:

1. Personality.

2. Social proof.

3. Urgency.

4. Trust.

First point:

You don't need to have all four in every single email.

You could.

There are only four. It's not that many. But it doesn't need to be a goal or anything like that. If you try too hard at this, it could become very technique-y. You'll lose some flow. And then it looks like you're just putting a bunch of tactics in your emails.

Looking at **personality**, which is the overriding one, this starts with authenticity. It's integrity. So you want there to be a flow to your writings that make them feel sincere and personal. And if you try to fill it with too many triggers it could be counter-productive in that sense. Personality you're using in every email to some degree. As for the others, let's say you use one or two of these triggers in an email, potentially three. And then sometimes you use all four. It just depends what you're working on.

The reason personality is a key action driver is because it's what makes your emails interesting. If your emails are flat, boring, and there's nothing that's unique or stands out about them, then why am I reading them? That's really the bottom line. You've got to have something that stands out about you that's specific to you and that shines through in this format. And that's where people will begin to develop a relationship with you and actually enjoy reading your emails.

So the idea is…

Put Lots Of Personality Into Whatever You Do.

That makes it fun and more interesting to read.

And little personal touches that may, for example, include live "look-ins" (when you share a little something that's going on in your life today as in 'I'm headed to the gym'). Little things like that. We live in a voyeuristic culture. Sprinkling in a little bit of live action is engaging and interesting to people. Don't overdo it. But adding "splashes" of personality is key.

Onto action driver #2: **social proof**.

We told a story a little bit earlier about T. Harv Eker and what he did with his fitness equipment store. Now this is obviously not a new thing. This is something that the restaurant industry and the club industry has used to a great extent for years and years. It can almost manufacture desire for their product or service offering. It may even trace back to P.T. Barnum and what he did to draw spectators to the circus.

The visual of there being a lineup outside the club or a lot of people in the restaurant is the effect you want to create. What you're conveying is other people do business with me and like it. That's essentially the message that we want to impart to the reader.

You'll do that in a number of ways. The most direct route is to share words of your customers. Testimonials are a very good example of what I'm talking about. That is one way to leverage the power of social proof, whether it's in written form or video form. You're letting your customers sell you for you. And that's inherently powerful as long as the testimonials are done right and are believable.

That's one version.

The other version is to just reference the plurality of people taking advantage of your offers and your service. For an author, a coach, or anyone that sells information on how to do something, even a line as simple as *all of my top students do this* can imply that idea. First, you're implying you have a lot of students. You have enough students that you have top students. And from your standpoint, you want to attract the best. You want the people who will self-identify with being a top student or committed or serious.

Even a simple statement like that will do it.

Another example is *since we've launched this, hundreds of customers have been rushing to sign up*. They're piling in, rushing in, breaking down the walls. Any visual you can create that makes it seem like there's momentum happening right now is something that's inherently engaging. And it speaks to the prospect's fear of missing out. But it also does what I said earlier. It reassures the reader that you are a person that others have already selected to do business with.

It's the same concept.

It shows…

You've Been "Pre-Selected" By Other Humans.

It's sort of like the *nerd dates cheerleader* secret.

There was a movie about this I think. This nerd paid a cheerleader to hang around him, and all of a sudden other girls were interested. Women are wired to be more attracted to a man they know has options with other women. And in a similar way that's also true for business. You've got all this business. You've got all this going on with other customers. And immediately, in the eyes of the prospect, it elevates your status and the status of your offers. It makes them more appealing over somebody else's.

Next, let's talk a little bit about **urgency**.

There's a saying that goes, "Nothing happens without a deadline." And in my experience, if you want your readers to take action based on your offers, urgency is a must.

It's not an option.

Don't Just Give Them A Reason To Take Action, Give Them A Reason To Take Action *Now*.

Otherwise, there are way too many distractions.

There are way too many other rabbit holes to go down and get lost in that will prevent them from taking the next step. Hopefully you're emailing them many times with an offer. Either way, if they've clicked away and gone back to their lives, they might not think about it again. You would have potentially lost the sale.

The easiest and most straightforward way to do urgency is to put deadlines on all your offers. So whatever you do, it should always have a deadline. Now, certain types of products or service offerings are not as obvious for putting deadlines on. For instance, if you offer a service and your front-end offer is a free consultation. It's sort of an evergreen offer. That's your intake process for your business. Urgency is a little harder to do in that case.

One way around that is you can tease a rare or valuable bonus. *If you book a consultation now you'll also get X.* And X pertains to whatever the content or the lesson in your email was. Or, share or tease a particular secret and say if you book your consultation by this time, you'll get the details of how to do this on the call.

Or you can do things that are more like "implied" deadlines.

> *If you book today* I'll do Y for you.

That's very different from saying...

> *If you book by Thursday at midnight,* you'll get Y.

But "if you book today" is more open. Oddly, leaving it open can sometimes be stronger. They wonder, "Did I miss this? Is it ending today?"

If you're a freelancer or a coach and it's a service where you're always prospecting for new clients, again, creating that urgency can be a little bit tricky. But one of the ways I've done it for myself is just reminding people that I already have a lot of projects on the docket. I'm booked several weeks (or months) in advance. And most people, once they decide that they want something, they want it right away. The bottom line then becomes, maybe I won't be able to start on your project for another three or four weeks. So book your consultation today and we can at least get the ball rolling.

You don't want to beat prospects over the head with this. Don't do it in every single email. But every once in a while you're just reminding them, *hey, I'm busy.* I'm in demand. It's an excuse to join the queue and it demonstrates social proof nicely – thus rendering your lovely self more desirable. And if a project has just come up for them, they want to get on it.

And they know you won't be able to start for four weeks. They'd better get on the ball.

That's the psychology of doing it that way.

Let's move on to...

The final action driver, last but not least [drum roll please]...is TRUST.

There are a number of ways that you can 'do' trust.

Any Form Of Social Proof Is A Trust Builder.

Use that to the max.

Case studies and testimonials can build trust and belief.

Here are a few other ways that you can do it:

Use a confession of some sort. This is like an admission of guilt, one where you admit you were not or are not perfect in some way. Talking about something that you've struggled with in the past, or hasn't worked for you (especially if it's something your market can relate to) is one way to do this.

Another is *say who your product or offer is* not *for*. For instance, "this is not for anyone who does not already have 5,000 people on their email list". That is sometimes known as inserting a qualifier. Qualifying builds trust because people tend to think their problems are special and there's no one-size-fits-all solution. Whenever you state clearly who something is for and who it's not for, that definitely ratchets up the credibility of your offer.

Another more subtle one is *tell them when not to buy*, or specifically under what conditions they should. Honestly, this could be its own chapter. It's the distinction between "selling" and giving them the chance to buy. The simplest way to put this concept into action is to use this formula:

"If You Want 'X', Then Do 'Y'."

More precisely:

"If you want [whatever benefit or to avoid pain], then do [whatever your call to action is, whether it's book an appointment or get my latest course, etc]".

Gary Halbert was big on this format because of what he called its "built-in credibility". Think about it, you're not saying no matter who you are, or whatever your circumstances. You're highlighting *if,* and following it up with specific criteria that calls out your buyers. It instantly makes it both more plausible and desirable to anyone who fits those criteria. It's amazing how much power to amplify believability is contained within that two-letter word.

Finally one of the best things you can do to boost the trust factor is *drop in a little candor*.

That means admitting up front what might be perceived as a flaw with your offer. Being straight about things like a low page count, poor quality video/audio, info being a bit dated, how it won't work for certain situations, and others that low-class, non-value-shopping customers might complain about will tend to attract good buyers and repel the tire-kickers.

Here's an example of what I mean, it's from an ad I did for a training video for baseball:

> Right off the bat, let's get one thing straight.
>
> If you're looking for pretty…with slick production values…this video is nothing fancy.
>
> This is pure, raw, unfiltered information that **transforms** hitters.

In fact, my partners and I agreed this information is so valuable (and so needed) that we've deliberately kept production costs low so that we can offer it to you at the best possible price.

That's how it's done.

The idea is to highlight your product's weaknesses, and almost spin them so they become strengths.

Chapter 9

Tips For Writing

"Your job isn't to find these ideas but to recognize them when they show up."
— Stephen King, *On Writing: A Memoir of the Craft*

If you'd like to learn a Marvel superhero trick to crush your competition, read on.

A while back, I took my daughter to see *Aquaman*.

I love superhero movies.

But lately I've felt a clear preference for ones produced by Marvel (e.g. The Avengers, Thor, Ironman, Black Panther) vs. the other of the big two comic book legacies: DC Comics. Aquaman is a DC Comics character. The movie was OK, but I kept thinking, "why is this just not as good as a Marvel movie?"

Fast-forward a few days. We hit the play button on *Avengers: Infinity War* which had recently come on Netflix. I knew the second I heard the first few lines of the script what the difference is…

WRITING!

Marvel has superior writing:

> *"Hear me and rejoice. You have had the privilege of being saved by The Great Titan. You may think this is*

suffering. No. It is salvation. Smile, for even in death you have become children of Thanos."

Quoted above are those opening sentences, which in the scene are pronounced magnanimously by the sorcerer Ebony Maw, as he steps over bodies in the wake of Thanos' attack.

It's not even that DC's writing is bad. It's not. But Marvel's writers have that slight edge that, when repeated throughout the film delivers a better experience. The jokes are just that little bit funnier. The story lines, just that little bit more imaginative. The dialogue, just that little bit cleverer. These are big, blockbuster movies. And even though, in my opinion, anyone who enters the theater is under an implied contract to suspend disbelief, the challenge for the writers (especially over several movies) is to keep one-upping themselves without it getting too…well, *wacky*. One way Marvel's writers get around this is by poking fun at the genre, as seen in this brief exchange:

Dr. Strange: *"If Thanos gets his hands on all six Infinity Stones he'll be able to wipe out life on a scale hitherto undreamt of."*

Tony Stark: *"Did you seriously just say 'hitherto undreamt of'?"*

It lets the tension out of the big scenes and keeps the audience on side with the characters.

Let's go to the scorecard.

Here's Marvel vs. DC by the numbers (domestically):

*Average gross revenue per release: $247M to $224M in favor of Marvel (keep in mind Marvel has produced almost double the number of movies DC has. Thus, higher output AND higher average.)

*Percentage of releases grossing over $200M: %58 to %48, again in favor of Marvel

*Opening weekends: Marvel, 6 of the top 15 (and 3 of the top 6), DC, 5 of the top 15 (highest at #5)

*Critically, Marvel movies tend to have many more favourable reviews than DC movies (with the exception of the three Batman movies directed by Christopher Nolan, those are truly special)

All this is despite DC having, arguably, more iconic characters – Superman, Batman, and Wonder Woman.

Internationally, Marvel is more popular as well.

What does this all mean for you?

Words matter.

If you had even slightly higher-converting words throughout your business (in your email newsletters, in your print ads, on your social media, in selling situations, in the scripts you give your employees – you do give them scripts, don't you?) not only would you be more popular in your niche, but you'd steal market share faster than a bandit in a Bugatti.

If you'd like to find out how email helps you convert more leads and sell more to your existing customers, go here to request your stress-free *Brainstorm Call*: conorkelly.com. Wipe out your *competition* on a scale hitherto undreamt of. Then, rest and watch the sun rise on a grateful universe.

Here are just a few more of my musings on how to reach into the dark recesses of your brain and pull out the most dramatic, interesting, curiosity-provoking and sales-boosting hooks to get the most out of any content program, whether it's email, blogging, social media, or otherwise.

Without further suspense...

When Stars Like Brad Pitt & Leonardo DiCaprio Crap The Bed

Behold:

During my brief YouTube career I was known as the "one-take wonder". Alright fine. I gave myself that nickname. But STILL, many of the charming videos you'd find on my channel were captured in their full glory on the very first take – with no rehearsal. There was, of course, one very notable exception ten years ago. On this day, it took me a full 90 minutes to capture a 4-minute intro video to our Fitness Bootcamp. I just couldn't get the words out. I was a total mess.

Why do I bring this up?

I recently saw a clip of Brad Pitt, Leo DiCaprio, and Margot Robbie where each of these great actors copped to the same thing happening to them at one point in their career...except with a hundred people on set, a famous director, and one day's production budget on the line.

Point being if it can happen to them...It can happen to anyone. You can let it get you down...or you can shake your head, get a self-entertaining smirk, go *wow that was bad*...and write an email to your list about it that makes you sales.

Exhibit A: About a week after my case of verbal constipation we put it on display by releasing a mighty humorous blooper reel that both got attention and garnered a new sign up. Also, note that here I am not so subtly going back to that well once more. As the saying goes, "nothing bad ever happens to a writer." Indeed, anything "bad" that happens to you can be turned into a story that sells your product or service. You can also use *others'* when-things-went-wrong anecdotes, per my shout out to the esteemed thespians above.

These types of stories are inherently interesting.

A Cheeky Way To Create Content On The Fly

Here's a good one.

If you're ever pressed for time or short on ideas, here's an easy way to drum up great content lickety-split. What is it? You simply quote an expert in your niche or industry and add your comments. Here's something CBC Radio Host Terry O'Reilly wrote in *Marketing Lessons from Under the Influence* which I think sums up the power of email marketing quite nicely:

> A well-timed nudge is a sophisticated aspect of marketing that is usually the exclusive domain of big advertisers. But small to medium marketers can also take advantage of nudges if you recalibrate your thinking to look for opportunities. There are endless reasons people don't buy an item, even though they are teetering on the edge of making a purchase. Often, I've said if the dealership had just called me one more time, I would have bought that car. Or if a store had thrown in the speaker wire for free, I would have bought that stereo. Or if the salesperson had spent five more

minutes with me, I would have bought two shirts instead of one.

OR [my words now]:

What if the restaurant, spa, yoga studio, chiropractor, or real estate agent had followed up with me in a format I find both useful and enjoyable – that I had chosen to receive – and enticed me to do business with them more often, when the time is right for *me?* If I liked the place would it make me a more active, loyal, and engaged customer? You betcha. There's simply no better way to do this than with the "drip marketing" of monthly, weekly, or daily emails.

By the way, did you catch what I just did there? I told you to quote an expert and add your comments then I quoted an expert and added *my* comments. Cheeky indeed. But you get the idea. This is an easy one to model.

Here's the best part...

Not only are you providing valuable insight, but your reader's brain unconsciously registers the idea as coming from you. In that sense, *as long as you give credit* you can legally and ethically borrow this great mind's credibility while riding shotgun on his/her illustrious coattails.

Chapter 10

More Best Practices

"I write only when inspiration strikes. Fortunately it strikes every morning at nine o'clock sharp." — Somerset Maugham

What is the most important line in any email?

I'll give you a hint.

It's NOT...

*your opener

*your subject line

*your call-to-action

Or even your link. Would you like me to tell you what it is? Ok, enough suspense. The #1 most important part of any email is...

The Sender's Name.

That's right.

WHO the email is from matters more than almost anything else. It's not that things like subject lines aren't important. Indeed, if you know your market well (and you should) there are ways to make your subject lines almost impossible to ignore – like an itch they simply have to scratch. But if your subscribers know, like, and trust YOU…THAT's what ultimately gets them to open your emails and devour your words like freshly baked cookies.

You see, intelligent email marketing is about the relationship. And relationships are like bank accounts. Every time you send a funny, inspiring, or personal note with a story, a relevant tip, or an interesting fact, you make a deposit. (One great thing about using email is it's easy to make regular deposits.) If all you do is pitch, pitch, pitch… or you're (gasp!) boring…or if your emails are about your product or service and not *your reader's problems*… you make a withdrawal. Then you risk your sendee losing interest or worse, tuning you out altogether.

On the other hand, when the relationship account is sporting a healthy balance, the people on your list who vibe with what you do will be delighted to see your name in bold when it pops up in their inbox. "More cookies, yay!" is what bubbles up from their subconscious. Then, not only are you welcome to send them more emails, but you can sell them more of your service or product via said emails.

See how that works?

That's accounting I like.

Remember, lead with a giving hand and you won't go too far from the mark. Before you hit send, ask yourself, "Will this serve in some way"?

The rest of this chapter will contain the ramblings of a mind obsessed with email marketing. It will drive home a few more important lessons. It'll bring together a few more best-practices to help your email marketing engage and sell like few others can.

How To Get Your Emails Opened Faster Than A Vegetarian Pizza At Al Gore's House!

Getting right into it, this next one is a doozie.

I'm going to share with you three subject lines that got high open rates and the psychology behind why they worked.

Here's why you should care: One client, a fitness boot camp, saw their average open rate go from 14% to 25% when I took over. On a 3K subscriber list, that's 300+ additional peeps reading your offers – *without any new marketing.*

No time to waste then…

1. Is Your Health Preventing You From Losing Fat?

I've used this one twice now and both times it was money. Whenever you can put contrasting ideas together it provokes a lot of curiosity. And curiosity is one of the marketer's most jealously guarded tools.

(If you look carefully, you'll notice ALL of my examples today have an element of curiosity to them.)

Back to contrast for a second. Jay Abraham likes to say, "Paradoxes excite interest." In this case I certainly mean 'lack of health'. But at a glance the phrase still does its job. How could health *prevent* you from losing fat?

You have to read it to find out…

2. Try this unusual health tip

Again, curiosity: what's so unusual about it? Also, anytime you can say 'try this' or hint at a tip of some kind, by implication there's actionable content inside. It's therefore perceived to be valuable. Once you have a proven winner, rip off or recycle that sucker with gluttonous zeal, as I did this one. "Try this unusual healing method" is a variation which also pulled an above average open rate for the client.

3. PRIVATE PHOTO: How to feel beautiful, right now

This one is admittedly tactical.

And stealthy.

People are voyeurs. We naturally yearn to be on the inside. That's one reason tabloids sell so well even though they're light on substance. Anything with the words *private* or *personal* will generally outperform most openers. So will adding *do not share* or *for your eyes only*. I wouldn't use these types of subject lines very often. And make sure whatever the hook is, it's paid off early in the body of the email. Don't leave 'em hanging, wondering where that dang private pic is. That'll erode trust. Other things being equal, sprinkling in a tactic here and there spices things up and keeps the interest high.

Go back and read this section a second time to let it sink in. There's a lesson to be found between the lines. Did you catch it? What am I doing here? I'm sharing valuable content, to be sure. But while doing so, am I demonstrating my expertise? Yes siree Bob. And by using client examples I'm invoking proof of my wordsmithing prowess. Unconsciously, you've accepted (a) that I *have* clients I do this for (which makes me credible) and (b) that they've gotten results, notably the instant, profit-boosting hit of more eyeballs on their emails.

I know, very "meta".

The lesson inside the lesson.

Next, discover:

What Is The Ideal Length For An Email?

Short answer:

As long as it needs to be.

Personally, I aim to keep them around 300 words or less – most days. Look, folks are busy. And a lot of them are reading your emails on their phone. By keeping things short and tantalizingly sweet, you train them to open your emails because they're not expecting some big commitment. That said I'm not against using 500-600 words if the message is good and it serves to do so. I just wouldn't do it very often.

I also want to make a distinction between *articles* vs. *emails*. I find many business owners are confused about this. Articles are content. The idea of email is to ask your customer to engage with you in some way, whether it's to reply, book an appointment, or click through to a longer piece of content that serves your marketing strategy.

I value CLARITY and SIMPLICITY in email (and other forms of copy).

Almost above anything else.

And I do like to do short punchy emails, because you should be able to get your point across succinctly. It's a good thing to do and a good skill to have. I'm also big on varying this so if I've done a couple of "longer" emails I'll split those up with a 100-200 word email sometimes. But more and more I worry less and less about length and focus on quality. What's most important is making your emails good, worth reading, and fun to read.

As long as you're keeping it about your market's problems and things they're interested in, it will be hard to lose them, no matter what the length of your dispatch.

The Right Type Of Honey To "Catch" Cold Prospects

I'm often asked, "Conor, any tips on using cold emails for B2B prospects?"

A few years ago I booked close to sixty talks at various companies by cold messaging HR people on LinkedIN. I was offering a free talk on health (which I'd then use to promote my services). HR people have a mandate to do a certain number of those, which I knew. And 'free'... well, the price was right. That's the simplest way I know to do it: straight benefit. Still, you have to play the numbers. Most people won't respond. I recently rebooted this practice for my business – and again, it worked. My revised 2.0 strategy for attracting cold prospects is twofold: (1) be utterly transparent, and (2) if you can, be *funny*. Both of those things defy expectations. And you want to stand out. A smile is a good reaction! Many people are too formal, especially when talking to high-level business execs, like they somehow lost their sense of humor when they became successful.

Your potential customers are human.

Don't be afraid to be human with them.

Still, the world can be a cold place – in business especially. Until they know about you and your wicked ways, the market out there is VERY cold. So what can you do? Simple...turn up the thermostat.

Allow me to explain:

I was recently asked how to sell to a resistant audience. And while my first reaction was I'd never sell to anyone who's resistant, I may have missed a beat in illustrating why – email. Nothing works better than email for "warming up" an initially reluctant prospect. You dangle a juicy bit of bait (something you know your market wants) and give it away free in exchange for an email address. Then, you follow up – endlessly. Until they either buy or unsubscribe.

The Chinese water torture...the drip, drip, drip of your unrelenting emails eventually brainwashes...er, I mean wins them over to your way of seeing the world. And by then the world is far less cold I assure you. That's when you get messages like (I'm paraphrasing, I've gotten many of these over the years):

Conor, you got me. I had my doubts at first, but slowly everything you're saying just started to make sense. And I'm not one for blogs or emails usually. Yours just hooked me somehow. When can we talk?

You heard it here first:

How to persuade even the most brow-furrowing, arm-crossing skeptic.

What If I Don't Have Much Of An Email List Yet?

What we're covering in this book will be of utmost value to anyone who already has a decent sized list of email subscribers. That said, I'm not against showing a little love to folks just starting out. After all, I was there myself once upon a time. When I started, I told everyone I knew I'm doing a free newsletter with fitness tips and did they want to be on the list. Start with people you know. Then, I collected emails at each of my talks, usually 20-30 at a time. That, together with leads coming through my website helped me build my list to 2,500 in less than three years. Also note: if you're a local business that sees customers every day, the fastest way is to get *them* to join your list!

Alright, next point…

Never Email While Under The "Influence"

I'll admit:

I get my jollies seeing these social media guru types and their shenanigans. So when one of this bizarre breed posted in my LinkedIn feed about "transparency" and "authenticity", I got to thinking...First, I fear those are becoming buzzwords and rapidly losing all meaning. Second, it's ridiculous that anyone would need help on how to be authentic. Third, he claims he's the *same guy* whether he's on social media, or with friends, or with the in-laws, or with clients.

Newsflash: that's not transparency.

That's *insanity*.

I'm no shrink but that might even make you a bit of a sociopath. Psychologists know well we all wear different personas. It's healthy. It's called being socially aware. It's true that as I get older, I'm less inhibited and more likely to speak my mind (and not give a crap about it either)...but there's still work Conor, Dad Conor, spending time with buddies Conor, on a date Conor, etc. If they were *identical* it would lead to some interesting outcomes I bet.

Besides that, what he's pushing is patently false. All of the big social media types are doing some kind of persona. Marketing gurus, celebrities, well-known business people – all have deliberate and well-managed public images (and they often pay consultants big bucks to help them with this). It's not that they're not being themselves; it's that they're amplifying certain aspects of their personality to suit the brand or image they've – key word – *strategically* chosen to create. Teach that. Not this other garbage.

Thus, let it be said The Muscle is not an "influencer". Don't be influenced. I'm a corruptor. Be corrupted. It's much more profitable, let me assure you. Mindless gurus like this – if you *let* them influence you – will have you spinning your wheels faster than a sports car in a blizzard.

Instead...

Create A Persona People Enjoy.

So says, ahem...*The Muscle*.

This doesn't have to be more complicated than putting the spotlight on selected parts of you (which are yet true to you...just maybe pumped up a bit for dramatic effect) and weaving this thread throughout the narrative of your marketing. Your personal uniqueness then becomes like a trademark that stamps all of your messaging and helps you stand out.

Besides, if you have to keep reminding everyone you're authentic, is that still authentic?

Alright, rant over.

Bottom line:

Never email while under the "influence".

Drug Dealing For Fun & Profit

True story:

The subheading above was the original title of Tim Ferris' famous book, *The Four Hour Work Week.* Not surprisingly, the publisher said "no way". So Tim took it to the court of public opinion. He used Google Adwords to split test book titles, and thus landed on the phrase that would ultimately brand the book's cover.

And, sure enough, the book was a runaway best-seller.

Similarly, here's a little-known way to probe and uncover your customers' most fervent appetites. Watch your open rates. I don't mean obsess over them, like some folks do. I'm well aware there are those who would cast doubt on the accuracy of open rates (Android phones have HTML turned off by default, they say). And your open rates will vary with the tides. If you add a lot of new subscribers, or start emailing more frequently, they'll most likely go down. I don't care about all that. I do think they're useful as a relative measurement.

Other things being equal, when a subject line gets a higher-than-usual number of opens, there's something to it. It may even be the smoke that hints at a wildfire of hot, flaming desire in your market. Not only can you reuse or recycle it, but it can help inform other marketing decisions as well.

Allow me to demonstrate. I had a client in the women's fitness niche who told me her highest ever open rate was for *Do You Want to Look like a Fitness Model?* So I said, "Run it again". And guess what? Same result. Sky-high opens. In theory, what could she do with said knowledge? Just off the top of my head (and this all should be *tested*)...

*Add "Look like a fitness model" as a slogan to her business cards

*Use that same question on flyers, postcards, and in other print advertising

*Test variations of the same in her Facebook or Google ads

*Say these words when talking to prospects on the phone or when meeting people face to face at a luncheon

*Take it a step further and create an 8-week program called *Look Like A Fitness Model* and sell it to her subscriber list

*And more

The point is open rates can be valuable intel.

When you know the words that make your market's eyes light up and their mouths water, your messaging becomes tighter and more impactful. You've got the right "drug" to get 'em hooked on you. This all can sound a little complicated if you're new to it.

Would you like me to handle this "marketing stuff" for you? Book your stress-free *Free Brainstorm Call* to see if you're a fit: www.conorkelly.com Discover your fun and profit (although perhaps not your 4-hour work week)....

The Howard Stern Method Of Dealing With Critics

Was rapping with an industry colleague the other day...

I subscribe to his email list. Recently, he'd sent a note to his readers asking for feedback and suggested topics. I *hated* it...even told him as much. Here's why: it's not my job to supply the theme-of-the-day. I'm a subscriber because I'm interested in what you have to say. I wanna know what you're passionate about; what inspires you. If you've got an opinion, I want to hear it. *That's* interesting. Not sanitizing your content so it appeals to everyone.

A listener once called *The Howard Stern Show* offering feedback, and Howard told him point blank, "not necessary." He went on to explain why a fan's critique is irrelevant, and how if he'd listened to feedback, he'd have quit a long time ago. "I don't care what you think, I care what *I* think," he told the stunned caller. This harkens back to what legend Matt Furey taught about email being like talk radio. Your "fans" tune into your "show" each time because they're curious about what you'll say next.

Here's another example:

I once attended a talk by fitness guy, Harley Pasternak. I thought most of his presentation was canned, catered to a general audience, and just plain vanilla (I personally like vanilla as a flavour, but the connotation is *boring* in case you missed it). It was basically the fitness equivalent of shoving a pacifier in the audience's mouth. But I liked the Q&A. Why? Because he dropped the niceties and plainly said what he thought. For instance, he called all the fuss about gluten "the biggest load of crap." I don't agree, but I sure appreciated hearing it.

Anyway, my industry friend received my comment in the right spirit. I think.

Here's the point:

No matter what you do, there's never been a time in human history that begged for honest, sober dialogue, more than this one. We're too afraid of offending, and too easily deterred by negative feedback. It's turning us into a society of wimps and whiners. Don't be one! Adding your voice to the chorus of mush out there might get you lots of likes on Fakebook, but it'll make you entirely forgettable everywhere else.

One of the most profitable exercises I ever did was part of the pre-work to a *4-Man Intensive* with the great Perry Marshall (by the way, I'd buy literally everything Perry puts out, it's that good). You had to list all your biggest successes from childhood onward, and talk about all of the various interests you've had at one time or another throughout your life. There was more to it of course, but this much was about really tapping into your uniqueness as a person. It was mining some of your most significant experiences. And apart from giving Perry some ammunition for what to talk about, it gave me pause to reflect on all the sides of myself I'm not showing, but could be.

No truer words have been spoken…

Your Customers Are Buying YOU.

First and foremost.

Figure out how you can be that…more…and in grander, glorious technicolor…and you'll be on your way to mastering this whole marketing thing in short order.

Another common question is about how to build an email list. I mentioned a few hints on how to do that above. Public speaking and web traffic (both paid and organic) were my main ones early on. Now I'm partial to joint ventures and barters. However, the details of this are beyond the scope of this book.

If you'd like to learn more, I created a custom product I call my **Evergreen List Builder** a while back to help my clients with the problem of consistently adding high-quality new leads to your subscriber list. And it's quickly become my most popular offering. It's not hard to see why. This is my answer to the moving target that is online marketing. I'll be honest, it's not the fastest way to build your list, but the leads are the highest quality.

Also, because my list builder is centered on *free* traffic, there's some sweat equity required on your part. Such is life. But if you're willing to put in a little leg work, the tools I'm going to provide you could be nothing less than a blueprint to double your business this year. My clients and me are using them to generate 50-200 new subscribers per month, for free. Not big numbers. But I'm talking quality buyers and customers. Go to conorkelly.com and reserve your *Free Brainstorm Call* to learn more.

Alright, last but not least.

As you prepare to leave the nest (sigh) and go off on the next leg of your email marketing journey…and before I wrap things up here…I leave you with this not-so-final yet all-important thought…

What The NBA Finals In 2019 Prove About Marketing

In 2019, The Toronto Raptors became NBA Champions.

Yes, Toronto is where The Muscle's secret lair is to be found. And yes, this victory pleases me [rubs hands together in a sinister way]. And no, despite the utter bedlam outside my balcony until the wee hours on the night we won, this will not be about that. This is about something that concerns you; something of big significance to any business. Here it is: tickets for Game 6 of the 2019 NBA Finals started at $935. That's a cool g-note to sit in the bleachers. And if you wanted to sit courtside to witness the Raps historic win? $16K. And let me ask you…if you were watching…did you notice any empty seats in that arena?

Here's the point:

THERE IS SO MUCH MONEY OUT THERE!

It's not even funny.

It undulates like a huge flowing ocean of yachts, sports cars and Prada bags. And if you're not getting as much of it as you'd like, you're only limited by your *imagination.* One of the best business books I ever done read is Dan Kennedy's *No B.S. Marketing to the Affluent.* In it, he describes how savvy business people are extracting exorbitant sums of cash from the market, eee gee:

- Sam's Club, which sells a **$48,000 wine tasting trip** to New Zealand – online
- He describes staying at Disney hotel for **$1,800 *a night*** – and notes only two suites were left
- Dean & DeLuca which offers a three-pound Candy Cane Christmas Cake – $135
- Love your doggy? Why not pick up a **leather dog bed** from PostModernPets.com for $1,450

These are just a few of literally dozens of examples in the book (and they get crazier). Few things will do more for your abundance mindset than to read it (and its companion *No B.S Wealth Attraction for Entrepreneurs*). I've read both several times. Instead of trying to figure out how you can afford to charge less, brainstorm how you can charge MORE, and simply add value. Money flows toward good offers.

That's where I come in.

You already do great things for your customers. My job as a copywriter is to tell that story so we build *so much value in your product or service* that it becomes a "no-brainer" for folks to do business with you…and to buy more, and buy more often. If you'd like to sell a whole lot more of something, more often, or sell it at a higher price, then let's hop on a no-hassle *Free Brainstorm Call* to find out if we're a fit. You could be a mere sales letter, email campaign, or website critique away from funneling a few swimming pools worth of that money ocean in your direction. Maybe even pay for one of said New Zealand wine-tasting trips?

In conclusion:

There is no scarcity; especially not when you put the right offer in front of the right people, using the right *words*. Believe in abundance, and abundance shows up. Use everything you've learned in this book. Put it into action without being attached to the response or feedback from any one email. Trust the process and KEEP. FRICKIN. GOING.

That's what I've done, and I assure you it's working out ok.

Finally, this is a short book. But it's packed to the brim with solid, proven information that will help any business in any economic climate. You want to own its contents. Go back and reread this sucker at least five more times. Each time will solidify the learning a bit more. Each time you'll catch things you missed previously. And with every re-reading you'll grasp the big picture even more – which is ultimately the idea.

Happy Wealth-Attracting,

Conor "Louis Vuitton" Kelly

Bonus Chapter

How To Hire A Copywriter

"What you say in advertising is more important than how you say it."
— David Ogilvie

Below is a sample of the "Consumer Awareness Report" I discussed in chapter three.

Go right ahead and model what you see here.

You will also learn the secrets to finding and hiring the ideal copywriter to help you grow your business.

Enjoy!

CONSUMER AWARENESS REPORT:

For Small Business Owners Who Are Serious About Growing Their Business…

Top Copywriting Specialist Reveals His "Insider's Tips" For Finding & Hiring The Ideal Copywriter For Your Business…Even If You've Been <u>Burned</u> In The Past!

Dear Biz Owner,

If you would like to know how to find and hire a good copywriter who can help you grow your business…and avoid being scammed or wasting time, energy, and money…then this report will show you how.

Here's the story:

As a freelance copywriter, I hear no end of horror stories from clients about previous copywriters they've hired. Many of them charge too much for low quality work…take forever to finish the project…and some so-called "copywriters" are…

Outright <u>Scammers</u> Who Will Charge You Big $$$ Only To Deliver An Obvious Swipe Job!

I'm not even joking about this.

It's gotten to the point now that I've heard so many of these "tales of copywriting woe" that I figure it's high time someone step up, call B.S. on the pretenders, and break down what a true professional copywriter does. With this report in hand, you'll be able to quickly identify who is "for real" and avoid being taken!

Without further ado:

FACT #1: Good copywriters…write (a lot)!

It seems like this should go without saying, but you'd be surprised how many copywriters don't write very much. Instead, they hang around in forums, or in Facebook groups, or pound the social media pulpit about some nonsense all these "guru" types regurgitate.

Lesson #1 is…

If a copywriter has more content on social media than on their blog or in books… that's your first red flag.

Real writers write. A lot.

You should be able to check out their blog (how often do they update it?), articles they've written, even books. Most of my copywriting clients became clients because they found my blog at www.conorkelly.com or joined my email list, liked what they saw, and got in touch.

The old adage, "if you want something done, give it to the busiest person you know" rings true in this case. You want a proven producer, not someone who just talks a good game. If you want your copy done, and done well, give it to the busiest copywriter.

FACT #2: Not all copywriters are *direct-response trained* copywriters.

There's a big difference between writers who provide content…even those who are copywriters for ad agencies that serve corporate clients…and a *direct-response* copywriter.

Note:

Direct-response marketing is <u>results accountable marketing</u>…and is the <u>only</u> type of marketing you should be doing as a small business.

That's a fact.

A direct-response trained copywriter has one job: to convert sales and customers for your business. That's it. Leave the "branding" to big companies with million-dollar advertising budgets. Your copywriter should deliver you more than just great writing.

I've been doing direct-response marketing for 12 years to grow my own businesses, and my clients businesses. This gives me real-life, tested, in-the-trenches experience to draw on that less experienced copywriters who are still "paying their dues" don't have access to.

If a copywriter can't tell you about their direct-response training, move on.

FACT #3: The best copywriters are also great marketers.

One way you can know this is by what they do to market *themselves*. If a copywriter sells their own books, products or courses and has their own email list in addition to taking on client projects…it's not a requirement…but it's usually a great sign.

Remember:

The success of any marketing initiative involves more than just copy.

There's strategy too.

That's why you want a *marketer* who can take ownership of the success of the project, more than just put words in print, or online. Being broad and well-read also helps. It gives the copywriter more to draw on in connecting ideas (which is what copywriting *is*…at its most basic level).

FACT #4: Dependable copywriters book in advance...and don't take rush jobs.

Good copywriters are *always* in demand.

There is a basic underlying reason for this: *every business needs more customers!* Copywriters who keep their word, are realistic about timelines, have a portfolio they can share, testimonials you can read, and are willing to let you talk to their clients, are harder to hire.

But that's a *good* thing.

One way you can tell is that they typically book projects in advance and refuse to take "rush" jobs. If I'm being honest, I can bang out a sales letter or a 10-20 step email campaign in a day. But it's the *research* that takes time.

And as you're about to find out, the research phase is critical...

FACT #5: The *right* copywriter for your business will ask the right <u>questions</u>.

I once heard a story of a client who connected with a copywriting "guru".

This guru said all the right things and sold the client one of his "proven" funnels. Charged him a pretty penny for it, too. It was a flop. The client acquired zero new leads and was left thousands of dollars in the hole. But what stood out to me about this story is that this guru did not ask the client any questions!

My sense is the funnel was something he "got lucky with" in another niche and foisted on this new client by simply swapping out the particulars. Legit copywriters ask a ton of questions. They drill down to the most infinitesimal details. They do an "unreasonable" amount of research because…

It's in the <u>research</u> that the real money is made!

The answers are in your market.

If a copywriter does not ask you a lot of questions about your business model, your market, or who your best buyers are (if you have any yet), be afraid…be very afraid.

CONCLUSION:

Well, that does it for this report.

There are some charlatans out there, it's true. The good news is, there are also reliable, high-quality copywriters who do great work for you that can transform your business almost overnight!

Remember, you're looking for a copywriter who writes a lot (and you can see evidence of it), is in-demand, asks a lot of questions about your market and your business model as a whole, and has both studied and mastered direct-response marketing.

If you'd be interested in finding out what it takes to hire me to do your email campaign or sales letter, here's where to start…

Book a no-hassle ***Free Brainstorm Call*** here:

http://www.ConorKelly.com

Once I know more about your business or your project, I'll tell you if it's a fit for me and if not I'll refer you on. Cool?

I'll be honest, I'm usually booking several weeks out (sometimes more) as I'm busy serving my retainer clients and with my own projects as well. And my services aren't cheap. (Although my clients would tell you my fees are fair…and not exorbitant by any stretch of the imagination.)

If we have a fit, and if you agree to my timeline and estimate, I'll send you a proposal that outlines all the important details of how we are going to drive a lot more dollars into your bank account!

Thanks again for reading this. And best of luck with your business!

To Your Success,

ABOUT CONOR KELLY

Conor Kelly is a leading copywriter, email marketing specialist, and publisher of the "Small Business Marketing" Newsletter. He also publishes daily marketing tips on his website at *www.ConorKelly.com* . He specializes in helping authors, speakers, and coaches sell more books, courses, and high-ticket coaching programs. His emails and sales letters are read by people all over Canada, The U.S.A., Europe, and Africa.

"I've been working with Conor on the sales page for my membership site and he's been outstanding. I've probably learned more from working with him on this project than in all the other marketing resources I've studied over the years. (Yeah, he's that good.) Which is why I recommend you to get on a call with him sooner rather than later!"

— **John "Coach Bru" Brubaker**, Best-Selling Author & Keynote Speaker

www.ingramcontent.com/pod-product-compliance
Lightning Source LLC
Chambersburg PA
CBHW071125240526
45465CB00024B/1189